Asking Rights

Why Some Nonprofits Get Funded
(and some don't)

By Tom Ralser

D1512224

For my parents.

Table of Contents

Preface i

General Introduction iii

The 100 Word Introduction v

The One Sentence Introduction vi

About the Author vii

Key Concepts ix
  #1 What are *Asking Rights*? ix
  #2 Outcomes are Correlated to Funding xii
  #3 A View from the Trenches, Not the Ivory Tower ... xvi

Section 1 Introduction 1

Chapter 1 The Investor's Perspective 5
  Time to Stop Ignoring the Investors 5
  How Investors Think 7
  Investors Demand a Different Approach 9
  Why Outcomes Matter so Much to Investors ... 11
  Investors and the Vagueness of Mission and Capacity ... 13

Chapter 2 Industry Disconnects 17
  How the Nonprofit Industry Disconnects with Investors ... 17
  Disconnect #1 Multiple Personalities 17
  Disconnect #2 Theory and Reality 19
  Disconnect #3 The Charity Mindset 20
  Disconnect #4 A Focus on the Wrong Things ... 22
  Disconnect #5 Perceived Inefficiency 23
  Disconnect #6 Misunderstanding ROI 24

Chapter 3 One Log Doesn't Make Much of a Fire ... 29
  Two Schools of Thought 29
  The Emotional Camp 29
  The Rational Camp 33
  Moving to Field Trials 34
  Where Does This Leave Us? 38

Chapter 4 Bus Drivers Eat Free 43
  Motivations Matter 43
  Two Separate Value Propositions Make it Confusing ... 44
  The Investor Motivation Matrix 51

Four Activity/Product Categories 53

Chapter 5 Why People Give 57
Why People Give: Conventional Wisdom 57
Why Do You Give: A Primary Experiment 62
A Summary... Maybe 68

Chapter 6 More Than Metrics 71
Numbers Alone Do Little 71
It Started with "Impact" 72
Some Movement Forward: Online Sources 73
Going Too Far? 76
Putting It All Together 78

Chapter 7 More Than Measurement 83
Evaluation is Not Impact, Measurement is Not the Point 83
Confusing Metrics with Value Propositions 87
ROI is Not the Same as Measurement 92

Section 2 Introduction 95

Chapter 8 Something Old is New Again 97
The Master is Still Relevant 97
Good Seats Still Available on the Bandwagon 102

Chapter 9 The *Asking Rights* Formula 105
The Genesis 105
Real World Examples 113
The Hypothetical Nonprofit 116

Chapter 10 The Investment-Driven Model and Investable Outcomes 119
Moving Beyond the Ingredients 119
The Investment-Driven Model 121

Chapter 11 Driving the IDM Further 141
One More Category 141
The MBO/FBO Comparison 144
Same Idea, Different Words? 146
Why is the IDM so Successful? 147

Chapter 12 Do You Have Asking Rights? 149
I Don't Want You to Hire Me 149
The Method to the Madness 153
Some Quantitative Evidence 158

What This Told Us   159

Section 3 Introduction   163

Chapter 13 It's Hard to See the Forest for the Trees   165
Why Are You Reading This Book?   165
Tragedy + Urgency = Immediate Rights (Usually)   166
Gadget Plays and Gimmicks ≠ *Asking Rights*   170
A Step in the Right Direction   173

Chapter 14 In the Trenches   177
Necessity Breeds Change   177
Serious Campaign Differences   178
Filling the Vacuum of Efficiency   181
A Few War Stories   182
Communicating Outcomes in the Real World   185

Chapter 15 What You Must Do Six Months Before You Ask   193
Step #1 Get Your House in Order   193
Step #2 Conduct the Nonnegotiable Feasibility Study   197
Step #3 Use What You Just Learned   199
Step #4 Use Campaign Dynamics / Launch a Campaign   201

Chapter 16 Takeaways   203
10 Things to Remember   204
A Bit of Levity   205

Index   209

Preface

When it comes to *funding* for nonprofits, what matters is NOT:

1. What the nonprofits themselves think; or
2. What "big hat, no cattle" consultants think.

What really counts is what the people who actually write the checks think.

Unlike a "normal" business, nonprofits do not derive revenue from those who purchase their goods or services. They do, however, have two sets of customers. Both are important to an organization, but *investors* are the customers who, in the end, allow a nonprofit to continue to operate.

This is ultimately a book about how to more successfully fund a nonprofit, including a perspective not normally discussed—that of the funder. The focus, though, is not on just any nonprofit; it is on those that deliver outcomes that are valued. The book will likely resonate with two distinct audiences: the nonprofit looking for sustainable funding and the investor in nonprofits whose opinions have been largely ignored. It is also a book about the nonprofit industry itself, and presents some time-tested methods on how to secure more funding at the individual organizational level. Most importantly, it presents a model that helps nonprofits more successfully do what they are supposed to do, which benefits everyone.

This book is written decidedly from a real world perspective. It is not written with hopes of literary awards or to make the old-school fundraising establishment happy; in fact, it is certain to ruffle a few feathers in the fundraising industry. But it's time someone stood up for the investor for every individual, business, or foundation that has ever been asked to support a cause and told the truth. Sustainable funding is not about glossy brochures, special event galas or fundraising software.

*It's about **earning** the right to ask people for money.*

When this right is earned, the "ask" is successful, funding flows naturally, and the nonprofit can continue to deliver on its mission in a sustainable way.

Most of the literature with the word "ask" in the title is purely focused on mechanical fundraising: how to structure, plan, and execute a fundraising solicitation. This book incorporates the view from the other side of the desk, that of the funders, which includes individuals, foundations, and corporations. It is not written from an academic perspective, where theory seems to win over practicality. I did not formally interview dozens of funders, like some "gurus" do, to simply collect their opinions for the sole purpose of writing a book. Those opinions are easily offered, and everyone has them. Instead, over the course of the last 18 years, I have interviewed thousands of funders in an actual funding context... with real organizational goals, societal issues, and critical projects at stake. Those who are willing to "put their money where their mouth is," are the people whose opinions formed the basis of this book, and whose opinions really count.

The following pages are a synthesis of the lessons learned from being in the funding trenches every day for the past two decades. In the beginning of my career, I witnessed the use — almost exclusively — of emotional-based appeals. I quickly learned this was primarily because emotional appeals were the only tool nonprofits had in their toolbox. But times have changed. People — people who invest in nonprofits — are smarter today. They are on to this type of emotional blackmail and, for many, it's counterproductive no matter how dedicated they are to the cause.

The evolution of the fundraising industry has been slow, but it continues to move forward. The goal of this book is to help continue that positive momentum.

General Introduction

Why *Asking Rights*?

It all started years ago when I was interviewing a banker in the great state of Tennessee as part of a funding feasibility study. We were in perhaps the largest bank in a small town, and his office was upstairs, lined with deep mahogany panels not unlike a judge's chamber. His desk was between us, and his outline was silhouetted against the windows behind him. At that point I noticed the particular nature of his appearance. He wore a white suit, which in itself was not unusual for a southern gentleman during that time of year, and his white hair was parted on one side. He had on thick, black-framed glasses and, to top it off, he was wearing a black string bowtie.

The comparison to Colonel Sanders of Kentucky Fried Chicken could not be helped.

We exchanged introductory comments and began going through the questions about the nonprofit in question. He was extremely cordial in his various responses, as I'd found many company leaders in the rural south to be. I directed the discussion for a good 40 minutes, finishing with an open-ended question designed to let him say whatever was on his mind. I hoped to uncover some additional nugget of information that I could use in the coming campaign. His response was measured and delivered with all the southern intonation he could muster: "Son, what gives you the *right* to ask me for money?"

His question was not directed to me personally, which will disappoint those who are still firmly committed to the old adage that "people give to people." It was directed instead to the nonprofit I was representing. They really had no relationship with the man. He accepted my request for an interview because, as a prominent member of the community, he was one of the usual suspects in the area.

His pointed question has never left me. It's what lead to the idea of *Asking Rights*, which is a two-word phrase that seems to encompass so much of what unsuccessful (from a funding perspective) nonprofits fail to develop and what successful nonprofits do. It provides purpose and meaning for a feasibility study. It is the pivotal underpinning for a nonprofit's quest to secure more funding. And without it, any and all fundraising efforts — for operating, capital, or endowment needs — will be less effective.

This accidental lesson has grown to influence much of what I do today, to the point where *Asking Rights* has, over time, become many things, such as:

- A 20-question quiz designed to help a nonprofit understand how much work needs to be done before it makes sense to hire my company to help them.

- A main theme or underlying current to almost every workshop, presentation or conversation in which I am professionally involved.

- The one question to which I must receive a satisfactory answer before I can agree to work with any nonprofit.

- A school of thought that challenges some of the most sacred of cows, entrenched practices, and old-school strategies in the nonprofit funding arena.

It is also, as you know by now, the title of this book.

The 100 Word Introduction

Nobody likes to see their hard earned money wasted. Yet when it comes to giving money to nonprofits, many people seem to turn a blind eye to the reality that not every nonprofit is a good steward with the money they are given. Not that they steal it, or that anything unseemly or illegal is going on, but that they are simply not impacting the world as the giver was led to believe. This lack of impact (or effectiveness), becomes most obvious when one is asking funders for money. That's when the real discussion takes place.

The One Sentence Introduction

It's all about the outcomes.

About the Author

Tom Ralser is a Principal with Convergent Nonprofit Solutions, which uses all of the tools available to successfully secure funding for its clients. Tom has personally worked with nonprofits in all 50 states on more than 500 funding projects, and his ROI-based approach has raised an estimated $1.1 to $1.6 billion dollars.

In his 18 years of working directly with local, regional, national, and international clients, he has sought to bring change, clarity, and improvement to the funding process. His first book, *ROI for Nonprofits: The New Key to Sustainability*, represented a major change in how to capitalize on the motivations of those who are most likely to invest in today's nonprofits. *Asking Rights* builds on that theme, outlining the necessary ingredients and processes to monetize outcomes and build truly financially sustainable organizations.

Key Concepts

#1 WHAT ARE *ASKING RIGHTS*?

Nonprofits have the legal right to ask you for money. Not all of them have *Asking Rights*.

The Internal Revenue Service (IRS) has granted nonprofits permission, or the privilege, to ask for financial support. Nonprofits actually have more legal leeway than complete strangers to ask you for money, since many cities have "No Panhandling" zones. They also, by definition, have an *obligation* to ask for money. Their tax-exempt status, and the laws they must abide by to keep it, requires them to seek external sources of funding. They are obliged to ask for help—for monetary help—to fulfill their mission and in order to survive.

So who do nonprofits target to fulfill this legal obligation? Individuals, corporations, foundations, trusts, estates, any level of government, and even other nonprofits. Requests for financial support are, in this day and age, almost expected by many of us. Think about the collection basket at church, the Girl Scout cookies our officemate is selling for his daughter, and the ever-present bell ringer that unmistakably heralds The Salvation Army's annual holiday appeal. Some of us give more than others; some of us never give at all. If we do give, it might be a cash donation, a check, a gift of property, or perhaps a distribution from our 401(k). In other words, virtually anybody or anything can be a conduit to funding. And even though nonprofits have the legal blessing to ask any entity for financial support, from the point of view of the askee, many nonprofits have not yet earned the right to ask for it. And this feeling is growing.

The nonprofit sector has made a science out of the study of the best ways to ask for money, and almost all of it is firmly planted on the emotional appeal side of the debate. There are hundreds of books and volumes of reports filled with the fundraising industry's "proof" that giving is a purely emotional act. There are scientific studies that show the act of giving excites a part of the brain associated with pleasure. There are well-done, statistically valid reports showing that most donors believe their nonprofit of choice does a good job with their money. It doesn't seem to matter to most donors that they don't really *know* if the beneficiary of their generosity is a good steward of their money. They simply believe that they are, and that's good enough for them.

Nonprofits learned long ago not to look a gift horse in the mouth. If a nonprofit can raise money based on emotional appeals, then why not? The system works. I have personally been in many a nonprofit's office, knee deep in their financials, and have seen firsthand that they spend more on brochure design than brochure content. The picture on the cover that elicits an emotional reaction seems to be far more important than the information inside, the information that demonstrates the value they deliver.

An interesting analogy relates the fundraising business to that of the diet business. There are thousands of books, DVDs, plans, programs, magazines, reports, and advertisements that purport to have found *the* one-and-only method of weight loss that will work for you. Alas, most are only a slight tweak on the same old theme, but that doesn't stop the endless stream of "new-and-improved" articles, books, plans, and so on. This phenomenon is so interesting because the magic formula is simple: if you take in fewer calories than you burn, you will lose weight; if you take in more calories than you burn, you will gain weight. If the formula is so simple and so easy to understand, why are so many diet books written and, worse, why are they bought?

The fundraising business as it exists today shares many of the same traits as the diet industry, including the fact that most studies and claims are only a slight tweak on the same theme: emotionally-based, personal relationship-predicated dogma that has been around for decades. So why are so many books on same-old, same-old fundraising bought? My guess is for the same reasons people think buying the latest-and-greatest diet advice will help them slim down more quickly: people want someone to tell them how to do it faster and easier. But that thinking ignores the simple fact that to lose weight—or to raise the needed funds—you still have to do the work.

To take this analogy one step further, most experts agree that a successful weight loss program involves a lifestyle change where old, bad habits are replaced with new, healthier ones. Sustainable funding for nonprofits is very similar. Earning the right to ask for money is also a lifestyle change. In locales where I have delivered workshops and seminars on sustainability plans, return on investment (ROI)-based funding models, and developing investable outcomes, the nonprofit community has adopted the language of the investor. But simply adopting a new vocabulary does not earn *Asking Rights*. Saying you will deliver outcomes — the impact you have on your primary customers' lives — that are valuable to the investors is vastly different, and more difficult, than actually doing it. In fundraising, walking the walk is much more important than talking the talk.

So, to answer the question "What are *Asking Rights*?" *Asking Rights* are:

> *The ability of a nonprofit*
> *to deliver outcomes*
> *that are valuable to investors.*

There are many operative words in this definition:

Deliver
> The nonprofit must actually deliver on its promise of results, not just print glossy marketing materials repeating its mission and goals.

Outcomes
> The results need to be in terms of how they impact their primary customers' lives, not just measures of activity that describe how the money was spent.

Valuable
> The outcomes need to be valuable in that they are meaningful to those whose investment made them possible.

Investors
> Those who make the intended outcomes possible through their investment. Investment, as opposed to gift, carries the expectation of performance.

The ability to deliver valuable outcomes is more difficult than it may sound. Every nonprofit, when asked if this is possible, will answer in the affirmative. Often, though, the outcomes they describe are not valuable to those being asked to write a check. In other instances, connecting the dots from funding to outcomes is terribly difficult. When the relationship between outcomes and value becomes too complex, funding suffers. It's actually an inverse relationship: as complexity goes up, funding goes down.

An even more important question is "Why bother with *Asking Rights*?" The answer is…

> *Long-term, sustainable funding for a nonprofit is best achieved by consistently delivering valuable outcomes.*

#2 OUTCOMES ARE CORRELATED TO FUNDING

The observation that the outcomes delivered by a nonprofit are directly related to its long-term funding is, to me, beyond question. However, much of the industry, as evidenced by its everyday actions, must believe that fundraising success and the outcomes of the nonprofit for which money is being raised are only distantly related. My belief of the correlation between outcomes and funding may, unfortunately, be an empirically unprovable relationship, much like the Laffer Curve.

The Laffer Curve is a theoretical representation of the relationship between tax rates and tax revenue raised. It is attributed to Arthur Laffer who, during a meeting with Dick Cheney and Donald Rumsfeld no less, reasoned against President Gerald Ford's tax increase by sketching his argument out on a napkin.[i]

The Laffer Curve is not provable, but its appeal to common sense is indisputable. Graphically, it looks like this:

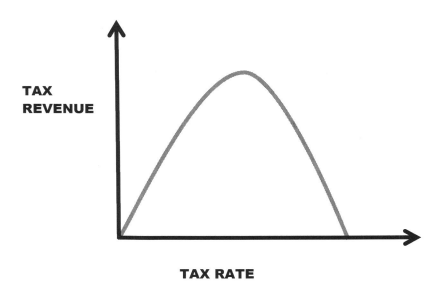

Logically, it follows this path:

1. At a zero percent tax rate, no tax revenue is generated. *Agreed.*
2. At a 100 percent tax rate no revenue will be generated, since why generate income if all of it will be taken away? *OK.*
3. There is a curve that represents the relationship between these two extremes, usually drawn somewhat symmetrically, and peaking at 50 percent. *Still with you.*
4. So, if tax rates go too high, at some point less tax revenue will be raised. *I'm listening.*
5. The tricky part is determining what exactly is the particular rate that maximizes tax revenue, or at what point do tax rates become so intolerable that other consequences come into play, such as earning income in another country or not reporting income at all. *Makes sense.*

Although the concept is intuitively appealing, it remains a theoretical concept. Estimates of this maximum rate, which hover around 70 percent, are controversial, and most agree that it is nonsymmetrical in shape, with the slope after the peak much steeper.[ii] But don't let the theoretical nature of the concept deter you from its applicability: the incentive to generate income on which taxes are paid goes down as the tax rate goes up, and at some point all of us would say "Why work?" if the rate gets too high.

What in the world does this have to do with fundraising? Even more important, what does it have to do with *Asking Rights*? The first Key Concept discusses the importance of delivering outcomes. Outcomes are one level beyond outputs, which are typically measures of activity. The relationship between delivering outcomes and the amount of money raised is predictable, just like tax rates and tax revenues. If I define that relationship as a positively-sloped line, increasing at an increasing rate, graphically it would look like this:

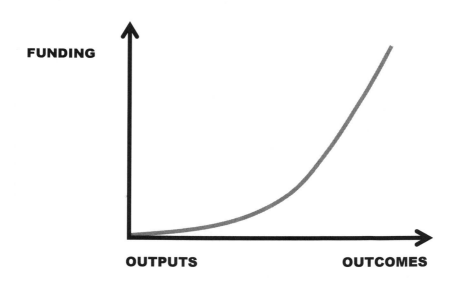

The logic follows this path:

1. When an organization only delivers outputs, they will raise some money, but be funded at lower amounts. Many organizations do this now.

2. As they move towards delivering true outcomes, the amount of money raised increases, though perhaps at a slower rate, since an organization's reputation for delivering outcomes takes time to build.
3. At some point, the organization's reputation for delivering outcomes, or more valuable outcomes, translates to increased funding at an increasing rate.
4. As long as the outcomes are valuable to investors, funding continues. In fact, funding may continue to grow even if the same levels of outcomes are delivered, since the reputation of the organization is so strong.

Is this relationship — for lack of a better term, let's call it the "Ralser Recurve" — as theoretical as the Laffer Curve? On one hand, I know funding campaigns are more successful when outcomes and their value are clearly articulated; we have decades of experience and hundreds of successful funding campaigns to prove it. This would indicate that it is not theoretical at all. On the other hand, some nonprofits raise a lot of money without ever delivering much in terms of outcomes. These organizations are typically "swimming in outputs," but do such a great job of marketing that nobody seems to notice. (My bet is that their salad days are numbered.) This leads me to believe not that the curve is theoretical, but that it is not universal.

Are outcomes related to funding? Absolutely. Just as an inferior product in the marketplace may enjoy some short-term success, market forces will prevail in the long run and either drive the price down or end demand for the product. How long that takes is subject to so many variables that estimating it is futile. That doesn't mean you should let the theoretical appearance of the concept deter you from its applicability. Similarly, as the nonprofit sector becomes more sophisticated, and nonprofit funders become more interested in the results of their investment, the relationship between outcomes and funding will come to be even more pronounced.

#3 A VIEW FROM THE TRENCHES, NOT THE IVORY TOWER

What if everything your outside fundraising counsel is telling you is wrong? What if your vast library of books and expensive training sessions are based on concepts that worked years ago but may not work so well today… or tomorrow? What if your local fundraising association is so entrenched in its own dogma that it can't change course for fear that it will appear foolish, or at least out of touch?

Look at the curriculum to become "certified" in the fundraising world. Look at the program of work your fundraising consultant is proposing. Look at how much time you spend on your gala, your race/walk, and your collateral material. Chances are, when you wash away the spin, the ambiguity, and the hype, these activities are all based on the assumptions that giving is purely emotional and that people give to people. Who makes these assumptions and advocates for these activities? Too often it is a person who has never personally made an "ask."

"But," say the professionals, "we have scientific studies to back up our claims that giving is an emotional act." Still others say, "I don't need to have personally made an 'ask' to know what works. I have worked with all kinds of organizations on their strategy, and they raise millions of dollars." Could these ways of thinking be self-serving, or at the very least, myopic?

Many nonprofits have bought into this line of thinking, which is based on defending the status quo, for years. It is a skewed version of reality and a good bit of bait and switch, which makes it scary to think that so many worthwhile nonprofits—organizations that are doing great things in this world—are continuing to perpetuate it.

For the sake of discussion, let's assume I am completely wrong. At the base of the discussion is a choice: either you believe that rational appeals (as opposed to emotional appeals) work or you believe that they don't. If rational appeals don't work, then you lose very little in believing that they don't and can go on your merry way, continuing to rely on emotional appeals in your day–to–day fundraising efforts. If rational appeals do work, then you stand to gain significantly by believing that they do, and potentially lose significant potential funding by clinging to emotional appeal orthodoxy. Therefore, it is not only practical and sensible to at least consider adding rational tools to your fundraising toolbox, it seems almost negligent to exclude them.

If you'll permit me this extreme example, my assertion regarding rational appeals is similar to Pascal's famous wager about the existence of God. He remarked, "I should be much more afraid of being mistaken (about the existence of God) and then finding out that Christianity is true than of being mistaken in believing it to be true." Pascal knew he could not convince true unbelievers of the existence of God through rational arguments. And, in fact, he was actually not arguing for the existence of God, but for the rationality of the *belief* in God.[iii] His aim was not to convert people to religion who were solidly against it, but to gain the attention of those who were skeptical... but still interested in hearing what he had to say.

Much of the same could be said about the concepts in this book. It will probably do little to convince the academics that a rational approach can be successful and/or perhaps even more successful than emotional appeals. My hope in putting pen to paper here is that it will capture the attention of those who are open to exploring an alternative approach, whether it's to add to their fundraising arsenal or out of necessity because the old approaches are not working so well anymore. My hope is that the people in the trenches who make nonprofits work—those who keep the doors open, often without the safety net of a national headquarters—will find these concepts the most useful.

In the same vein as Pascal, it is likely impossible to convince emotional believers of the value inherent in rational appeals by using rational arguments. *Asking Rights,* though, is based on what has proven to be successful over and over again, offering the critical link between theory and practice.

REFERENCES

[i] "The Laffer Curve," *Wikipedia*, Retrieved July 2013, from http://en.wikipedia.org/wiki/Laffer_curve

[ii] Don Fullerton (2008). "The Laffer Curve." In Steve N. Durlauf and Lawrence E. Blume, *The New Palgrave Dictionary of Economics (2nd ed.)*, 839, Retrieved July 2013, from http://en.wikipedia.org/wiki/Laffer_curve

[iii] Jeremy Stangroom and James Garvey, *The Great Philosophers* (New York: Metro Books, 2007), 47.

ASKING RIGHTS

Section 1 Introduction
Understanding Asking Rights

The predominant theme of existing literature about funding nonprofits centers around how to wring more money out of individuals, foundations, corporations, and the public sector through emotional appeals, peer pressure, and slickly crafted marketing campaigns. While sometimes effective, encouraging nonprofits to pursue these efforts can actually be counterproductive. These practices do not serve the nonprofit sector well in the long run because they focus attention away from the true value that nonprofits deliver.

The chapters in this section will move from describing nonprofit funders in the traditional way—as "donors" who "give" to a "charity"—to "investors" who "fund" valuable outcomes. Different schools of thought on emotional versus rational appeals are explored, as is why rational appeals are gaining more traction on the road to sustainable funding. All of this is a prelude to the second section, which explains how to use this information to develop *Asking Rights*.

This section is divided into three parts, each designed to provide the background necessary for effective *Asking Rights*.

Part 1 Understanding Today's Nonprofit Investor
    The Other Side of the Desk

    Ch.1 The Investor's Perspective (You know, the one that counts)
        Don't ignore your most important supporters

    Ch.2 Industry Disconnects
        How the nonprofit industry alienates investors

Part 2 Understanding the Motivations of a New Environment
    There Is More to It Than Just Emotions

    Ch.3 One Log Doesn't Make Much of a Fire
        The need for more than a single, emotionally-based approach

Ch.4 Bus Drivers Eat Free
Motivations matter (but not necessarily those you think)

Ch.5 Why People Give
New takes on conventional wisdom

Part 3 Understanding the Value of Numbers
Numbers Matter, But Only the Right Numbers Develop
Asking Rights

Ch.6 More Than Metrics
Numbers by themselves do not earn Asking Rights

Ch.7 More Than Measurement
Measurement is no substitute for management

Terms in This Chapter

Investor (often incorrectly identified as donor)

A type of nonprofit funder who is looking for a return on his or her investment (often incorrectly referred to as gift or donation). Although the term is more indicative of the mindset rather than the amount of money involved, an investor typically makes larger financial commitments that span several years. An investor is most concerned with the long-term success of the nonprofit.

Funder

A broad group — including donors, investors, grantors, sponsors, and members — that financially supports a nonprofit.

Donor

An individual or organization that typically provides low-level (definition varies by nonprofit size, budget, funding model, etc.), often sporadic financial support that is not necessarily connected to the mission of the nonprofit.

CHAPTER 1

The Investor's Persp
(You know, the one that counts)

Capital will always go to where it is well treated.
- *Wristons's Law of Capital*

TIME TO STOP IGNORING THE INVESTORS

Yes, *investors*. If you think you have picked up the wrong book, you have not. This *is* a book about nonprofits. But it uses a vocabulary that the funders of nonprofits understand and appreciate, not words that only those in the nonprofit arena understand.

The view from the other side of the desk, that of the nonprofit funder, is often very different than the perspective of the nonprofit itself. The broad category of funder can include donors, grantors, sponsors, and members, to name a few. Donors, in particular, are typically defined as those giving at the lower financial levels, although that level is subject to interpretation. No matter what label is put on a nonprofit funder, the reasons they financially support nonprofits vary widely and can encompass many motivations, demographics, and financial situations.

Nonprofit *investors,* on the other hand, have much more narrow focus than those of funders in general. They also seem to share a set of similar characteristics, tend to be rational thinkers, and respond to funding requests in a very different way than the broader population of funders as a whole. I define an investor as a certain type of nonprofit funder. They are typically willing to make larger financial commitments and possess a knack for long-range vision. A person who can only afford to donate time can also adopt an investor's mindset, and is considered an investor in the broader definition of the word.

A nonprofit investor, like any investor, is concerned
with a return on that investment.

The more that return is demonstrated in a credible way, the more money flows to the nonprofit. Exactly how the return on that investment is defined is a deeper discussion, and what much of the following chapters detail. At this point, let it suffice to say that one size does not fit all, but the closer we can get to putting a dollar sign, a percentage sign, or somehow quantify this return, the more successful the funding effort. Even if "what's in it for me" is only that warm glow someone receives from the act of investing in a nonprofit, it needs to be spelled out and communicated.

Donor is still, I'm sorry to say, the prevalent term. It certainly is a softer, more generic term that can describe anything from a few cents in The Salvation Army's holiday bucket to a multi-million dollar campaign pledge. The term *donor* is more focused on the act of giving than the mindset or motivation of the giver. When I started working in the nonprofit industry in the early 1990s, the term *investor* was not only unpopular, it was publicly ridiculed. While *investor* is still very much underutilized, it is getting more traction and gaining some respect... for good reason.

To expand on how the vocabulary can make a practical difference, the term "gift" is actually more inappropriate for the state of nonprofits today than the term "donor." Yet almost every book on traditional fundraising has "major gifts" in the book title, a chapter title, or gives it plenty of ink in the body of the text. As I mentioned in my first book — *ROI for Nonprofits: The New Key to Sustainability* — the word "gift" implies all of the wrong things and actually detracts from the concept of an investment in a nonprofit.

The good news is that the investor movement is growing, especially with the larger check writers. Some examples over the past several years include:

CBS News, *Charity As An Investment Goes A Long Way*[i]
"They are part of a growing trend in philanthropy — people who view their donations not only as gifts, but as investments."

The Economist, *Face Value: The Brand of Clinton*[ii]
> "Mr. Clinton . . . does espouse a businesslike approach to giving money that is now fashionable among the new rich. He calls these philanthropists 'bleeding-heart cheapskates': they are 'not naïve, they don't want to waste a lot of money, they like low administrative overhead, they measure pretty ruthlessly for return.'"

Chronicle of Philanthropy, *Increasingly, Companies Seek to Tie Giving to their Efforts to Achieve Business Goals*[iii]
> "More and more, charities seeking support from America's largest corporations must sell companies on the argument that working with them makes good business sense."

The Wall Street Journal, *World's Richest Man: 'Charity Doesn't Solve Anything'*[iv]
> Carlos Slim stated that he could do more to help fight poverty by building businesses than by "being a Santa Claus." He said "the only way to fight poverty is with employment. Trillions of dollars have been given to charity in the past 50 years, and they don't solve anything."

HOW INVESTORS THINK

How *investors* think can be summed up by the following:

> *If you can't demonstrate results (outcomes),*
> *then you do not have the right to ask for money.*

> *If you can't make your outcomes meaningful to me,*
> *then you do not have the right to ask me for money.*

This type of thinking is not only radical to those who are entrenched in the traditional, emotionally-based methods of nonprofit fundraising, it is generally off-putting to many in the nonprofit arena. Sometimes the reaction comes from a more personal place, involving the feeling that this type of thinking reflects improper protocol or an obvious lack of decorum. If you find yourself thinking that the phrases above are crass, cold, or unfeeling, then you are probably somewhat altruistic and believe that the good work done by nonprofits shouldn't be questioned. In other instances, the reaction is one of industry inappropriateness: these phrases are for-profit oriented and simply do not apply to nonprofits. Or, if you find yourself thinking that these phrases are too corporate, too bottom line, or too capitalistic, then you are firmly in the traditional camp that believes nonprofits and for-profits are separate universes, and any co-mingling of processes, methods, or practices is blasphemy.

The differences between how donors and investors think can be subtle to those not in the nonprofit industry, but obvious to a fundraiser who needs the most effective means possible to generate capital for a client. How these two groups think differently in certain important areas is illustrated by the following:

1. Need for Funding

    A Donor Will Ask
    Have you demonstrated the need for your services?

    An Investor Will Ask
    How will funding your organization improve the situation?

2. Approach to the Problem

    A Donor Will Ask
    Does your approach to addressing the problem fit within our giving guidelines? Is the problem you are trying to solve familiar to us?

    An Investor Will Ask
    Does your approach to addressing the problem make sense?

3. Funding Level

    A Donor Will Ask
    Have we sufficiently spread our available funding across those organizations addressing the problem?

An Investor Will Ask
Is this the right amount of money for your organization to bring about real change?

4. Measuring Success

A Donor Will Ask
Have you completed your report according to our guidelines?

An Investor Will Ask
How will you communicate your impact to me?

5. Delivering Results

A Donor Will Ask
What activities did you undertake to address the need?

An Investor Will Ask
What results (outcomes) did you deliver, and how do they improve the lives (alleviate the problems) of your primary customers?

INVESTORS DEMAND A DIFFERENT APPROACH

Like the southern gentleman I spoke about in the Introduction, every community has the usual suspects who are targeted by nonprofits for funding. In our company's engagements, while we may often approach these same people, we make that approach with a radically different set of tools that are ROI-based.

Below are common funder sentiments I have heard over the years. If you find yourself saying, "I've often felt the same way," take comfort in knowing that you are not alone. You've just discovered that you have an *investor* mindset.

"I hear the same thing from every nonprofit in town: We are doing great things! That is why you should give us your money."

"I've often wondered if nonprofits spend all day trying to figure out the best way to tug at my heart strings."

"Do nonprofits hit me with these emotional appeals because they have nothing else to offer? I would like to see some results before I give any more money."

Investors demand a different approach because for them the act of giving money is not necessarily based in emotion; it's more of a rational decision. This idea runs counter to the conventional wisdom of the industry, which feels that "giving is an emotional act."

To be clear, investing in a nonprofit is not exclusively a rational decision either. Being successful at securing funding from investors requires a fundraiser to address a completely different, nontraditional and, at times, often non sequitur set of motivations. It also involves a lot more homework.

Given the current global economic situation and the fact that slow growth is considered the optimistic scenario for the foreseeable future, understanding what works to capture investor capital may be the best possible strategic plan for nonprofits to deploy. In August 2011, for the first time in history, the AAA bond rating of the United States was downgraded. This was quickly followed by a major correction in the stock market and a nasty debt ceiling debate in Congress. All of these events are helping to form the perfect storm for less social sector spending — including pass-through spending for state and local programs — by the federal government, a change that will likely last for years to come and be partially irreversible.

The nonprofit sector will feel the weight of this situation through an increase in demand for services by our communities and neighbors in need. Some of this pressure will be due to predictable demographic shifts such as our aging population, which is directly attributable to today's longer life expectancies. But an even larger impact will be felt as nonprofits step in to fill the gap formerly financed by the public sector. This pincer movement of decreased funding and increased demand will undoubtedly force a game-changing paradigm for nonprofits, one that focuses on developing *investable outcomes*.

WHY OUTCOMES MATTER SO MUCH TO INVESTORS

The results produced by a nonprofit are the reasons
people give them money.

The statement above is true, whether you use *results produced*, or you substitute my preferred term of *outcomes delivered* in its place. I truly believe this, no matter how it's stated, but there are many in the nonprofit industry that do not.

This disagreement likely stems from the well-entrenched fundraising industry itself. Much of the curriculum, many conferences, and even some academic research pays homage to the previously mentioned "giving is an emotional act" mantra. One of the most widely quoted statistics in support of the emotional approach is that only 3 percent of donors care about results.[v] The shortcomings of this statement are discussed later, but the operative words — donor and results — are what allow a misleading conclusion to be drawn.

Those in the nonprofit industry who tout the emotional appeal approach also often choose to believe that running a nonprofit is *so different* from what outsiders — those shallow, clueless for-profit people and organizations — are familiar with that the idea of having to prove results to them is pointless. This attitude sends a pretty harsh message to the outside world; it signals that a nonprofit is above reproach. Furthermore, some of these nonprofits feel that adopting an ROI paradigm could even compromise their mission. Put more simply, the nonprofit world seems to be saying that even though you made your money in the highly competitive, for-profit rat race, you still don't know much about operating a nonprofit business and therefore don't need to be informed about how the mission is accomplished. So please, just give us your money and then go away. Thank you very much.

Reality is a bit different. Almost universally, people want to see their investment in a nonprofit do good things. And categorically, no one wants to see their money wasted. So how is a nonprofit investor, if they don't know enough about a nonprofit's business to understand how to gauge its effectiveness, supposed to know if their investment is doing what it was intended to do? In short, they can't. And if the nonprofit doesn't tell them, they'll never know… and will likely never invest again. Since there is no market metric — such as profit, share price, earnings per share, market share or price/earnings ratio — it is incumbent on any nonprofit that receives funding to clearly, consistently and concisely communicate with investors as to how their investments are performing.

If you are an investor reading this book you are probably thinking:

- How will the nonprofit's outcomes benefit the community?
- How do I measure the nonprofit's impact?
- Can the nonprofit's impact be objectively validated?

If you are a traditional, old school nonprofit, you are probably thinking:

- Our results benefit everybody.
- Our mission is not easily quantified.
- Our impacts take years to be fully realized.
- We can't put a price tag on someone's feelings.

The rub is obvious. Investors want to help, but they also want to be treated like investors. Not in name only on the annual report, but through honest, open, frequent communication as to how their investment is performing. Nonprofits by and large do not purposely withhold information that investors want, they just don't always know how to explain it. The reasons for this lack of interaction with investors is as different for each nonprofit as their missions are from one another. But as an investor once mumbled to me, "They can't help it; it's how they were raised."

INVESTORS AND THE VAGUENESS OF MISSION AND CAPACITY

Investors are familiar with mission statements. To many, mission statements are just words on paper, the result of lessons learned from the for-profit world. Case in point, I offer the two following ironic examples:

> *Our mission it to build unrivaled partnerships with and value for our client, through the knowledge, creativity, and dedication of our people, leading to superior returns for our shareholders.*
>
> – Lehman Brothers

> *Respect, integrity, communication, and excellence.*
>
> – Enron

While the history books will not be too kind to these two organizations, the bar for mission statements in the nonprofit world is even higher than that of for-profits because nonprofit mission statements are held as the embodiment of why an investor is being asked for funds. It is supposed to provide clarity of purpose, direction when in doubt, and offer daily motivation to the entire organization. In short, an effective mission statement is not *what* the nonprofit does, but the difference it makes.

Using industry jargon, when a nonprofit is doing what it is supposed to be doing it is said to be "fulfilling the mission." Outside of the nonprofit arena, "fulfilling the mission" comes across as vague and even a bit esoteric. So herein lies part of the problem. Nonprofits have their own vernacular, rules and "best practices" (a concept that proves once again the industry's overtly self-serving nature), but derive funding from those *not* in the industry. (This is related to the dual value proposition, which is discussed in a later chapter.) This behavior begs an interesting question: Doesn't it make more sense to speak the language of those your organization depends on for funding, instead of forcing them to learn your jargon-laced vocabulary, which may confuse or even offend them?

One of the more over-used words in nonprofit jargon is "capacity." Capacity means little to an investor. In fact, the definition of the word is even up for debate within the industry. Generally, capacity is a measure of the resources, skills, and processes that an organization has to address a given challenge. In fundraising terms, it is the ability of an organization to achieve its desired goal or outcome.

The word "capacity" is even broken down by industry consultants into subparts: structural, functional, and implementation. Do these further details matter to nonprofits as they search for realistic goals, engage in strategic planning, and structure their resources for success? I'm sure they do. Are they understood by potential investors? Possibly. Have I ever discussed them in a fundraising context? No. Not in 18 years.

REFERENCES

[i] CBS News, "Charity as an Investment goes a long way," 11 February 2009.

[ii] "Face Value: The Brand of Clinton," *The Economist* (Sept 22, 2007): 84.

[iii] Noelle Barton and Caroline Preston, "Increasingly, Companies Seek to Tie Giving to their Efforts to Achieve Business Goals," *Chronicle of Philanthropy,* August 7, 2010.

[iv] "World's Richest Man: 'Charity Doesn't Solve Anything'," *The Wall Street Journal,* October 15, 2010.

[v] "Money for Good: The U.S. Market for Impact Investment and Charitable Gifts from Individual Donors and Investors," Hope Consulting, May 2010.

Terms in This Chapter

Capital Campaign

A term traditionally used to describe fundraising campaigns for buildings or facilities. This is likely the result of the influence of the accounting profession, where buildings would be categorized as depreciable, capital assets. In this book, capital campaigns take on a larger meaning, referring instead to large dollar campaigns with multi-year pledges.

Outputs

An intermediate measure of progress, typically focused on areas of staff activity and things that are easily quantifiable, such as number of people through the door, total amount of products/services generated, hours volunteered, etc.

Outcomes

The impact a nonprofit has on its primary customer's life. This is to what end outputs hopefully lead. Outcomes can be much more difficult to quantify, hence the common habit nonprofits have of only reporting outputs, with the hope that they will suffice.

Primary Customer

The person or persons whose lives are directly affected by the work of the nonprofit organization. This is in contrast to a supporting customer, such as a volunteer, funder, staff, or board member.

Return on Investment (ROI)

A for-profit term that has recently found traction in the nonprofit arena. It is used to describe the value delivered for the amount of dollars expended.

The Ask

The activity or process of asking for money.

CHAPTER 2

Industry Disconnects

Nonprofit should be nonexistent - the term, not the type of organization. The time is right to insist on a term that focuses on the investment, risk taking, and entrepreneurial imagination that have always been so essential to organizations that serve the social good.
- Claire Guadiani

HOW THE NONPROFIT INDUSTRY DISCONNECTS WITH INVESTORS

The nonprofit industry, whether by design or by accident, seems to want to set itself apart. Differentiation is good, but only to an extent. As we've seen with the words "donor" and "gift," differentiation can create unintentional barriers that hinder an effective fundraising effort. While there is a small, innovative group of both funders and organizations that completely embrace the concept of nonprofit investment, the vast majority in the nonprofit arena have chosen not to change with the times.

This choice, which is perhaps as much the product of inertia for some as it is intentional for others, is puzzling because investors have consistently — loudly and clearly — voiced concern over the years that the nonprofits that ask them for money seem to be disconnected from the real world.

I have distilled these often heard comments into six distinct categories.

DISCONNECT #1 MULTIPLE PERSONALITIES

It appears to investors that many nonprofits want to say they are different from for-profits when it's convenient, and yet act like for-profits when it suits them. This is probably most apparent in the activity of fundraising.

The story goes something like this…

There are always the usual suspects in a local capital campaign, no matter where in the country one is launched. These are the same people, foundations, and companies that are approached time and time again for money. Because they are approached so often, these funding sources have become proficient at dissecting the ask. Having worked in the same geographic area on more than one campaign simultaneously, I have personally heard "Who do you want money for this time?" and "How much do you want this time?" uttered more than once by frustrated potential funders.

These usual suspects have been hit with every appeal known to man, most of which are emotionally based or follow the belief that an ask is more effective if the funder is approached by a friend or someone with whom they have a personal relationship. Because these go-to funders have seen so many different approaches, and so many one right after the other, they have developed a unique perspective that has crystalized into the conclusion:

> Because nonprofits spend so much time and money on trying to craft the perfect emotional appeal, they are doing nothing different than a for-profit would do when it attempts to market a product. Just like a for-profit hires an ad agency, a nonprofit hires a fundraiser.

The resentment these go-to funders feel towards this sort of behavior is rising quickly, and many view it as a slippery slope for the fate of nonprofits in general. When they do give money to a nonprofit based upon its carefully crafted marketing message, the momentary altruistic euphoria quickly turns to disappointment and disillusionment when the results promised by the slick collateral don't materialize or are not communicated well. Essentially, they feel duped.

How does this play out in the long run? It creates a cycle that does not bode well for the nonprofit that relies on annual campaigns to sustain its operation, when each year's appeal must be more intense than the last. It also raises the bar for all nonprofits to find more effective fundraising methods.

DISCONNECT #2 THEORY AND REALITY

As in most industries, there is no shortage of opinions from experts sharing their insights on the best way to do things. The nonprofit industry, however, seems to have more of them than many other industries. The nonprofit sector is unique in that it is not always easy for the real world to validate the results, therefore consultants who are not necessarily good at what they do can continue to find new clients.

Those that can't do, teach.
Those that can't teach, teach teachers.

This leads to a bit of editorial comment on the nonprofit consulting industry. Many of these well-meaning experts do more harm than good. These are the people who either say they can do things but really can't, or promote a nice-sounding theory of how nonprofits should do things but are so removed from the realities faced by the average nonprofit that they are often nothing but an expensive distraction. These are the "big hat, no cattle" types referred to in the first sentences of the Preface. They tend to overcomplicate things, use consultant-speak, and make recommendations that are unverifiable as to their effectiveness in moving an organization forward.

These actions sometimes even damage a nonprofit beyond repair. A fundraiser who convinces a small nonprofit that it should hold another fun run, because it works so well for the national nonprofits, is not helping the local organization in its quest for long-term financial sustainability. An academic who conducts seminars on fundraising, whose only hands-on subject matter experience has come through attending cocktail parties for his/her educational institution, only serves to make nonprofits — and funders — more wary of fundraisers in general. Some of these "experts" would be very hard pressed to actually put their theories into a structured fundraising effort, which is what we — who actually pound the pavement and knock on doors for clients — commonly referred to as a campaign. If all of this sounds a bit salty, it is based on personal experience. I have seen it too many times and am embarrassed by it.

Now, the other side of the coin. Robert Penna wrote a wonderful book on outcomes entitled *The Nonprofit Outcomes Toolbox*. It contains a wealth of knowledge on the specific topic of outcomes and is one of the few books out there that can be translated into practice. From a funding perspective, though, the question becomes how effectively can it be translated into sustainable *funding* for the typical nonprofit? In many circles, it is difficult to put theory into practice, much like the difference between taking an art class and becoming a true artist or reading a book on management one day and becoming an effective manager the next.

The bottom line of Disconnect #2 is... how many of these self-proclaimed experts have actually put their names on the dotted line to raise X amount of dollars—for a nonprofit, not themselves—based on their theories or observations?

DISCONNECT #3 THE CHARITY MINDSET

Charity, as a concept, is powerful. Charity, as a word, has too much societal baggage. Charity, as a business model or industry description, is an impediment.

According to Dictionary.com, charity is defined as:

1. Generous actions or donations to aid the poor, ill, or helpless; and

2. Something given to a person or persons in need.

It is obvious that these traditional definitions don't fit with many nonprofits, the work that they do, or the outcomes they deliver. Many nonprofits don't help the disadvantaged, and many don't even work with people.

The word charity is often closely followed by the word gift, which is what is given by a donor. But a gift, in its purest context, implies giving without the expectation of something being given in return, which is not the point of view of an investor.

Charity in a religious context is also not intended to be a part of this suggested paradigm shift. To paraphrase Ron Paul during one of his political speeches on the 2012 campaign trail, "True charity, in the Christian sense, does not need a middle man." Many mainstream religions hold charity as a virtue, and this belief is not being challenged. There need not be a fundamental split between capitalism and Christianity, or any other religion, where giving based on compassion for the necessities of life may even be considered a duty. To the contrary, I am challenging the belief that positioning a nonprofit as a charity, or anything even close, is actually a detriment in the quest for sustainable funding.

The most in-your-face version of this sentiment is a graphic produced for one of my former companies, ROImetrix, as seen in Exhibit 2.1. This international symbol for "no" — the red circle with a slash — is also now on the cover of a book, with the word fundraising instead of charity superimposed. I guess this qualifies me as one of the original "sell your impact, rather than beg for charity" pioneers.

Exhibit 2.1 No Charity

The point is that referring to a nonprofit as a charity, in a synonymous context, is exactly the wrong message to send to the funding public. As you might imagine, this line of thinking has gotten some interesting reactions over the years, but most have been in agreement.

An appropriate take on "charity" is offered by The Committee Encouraging Corporate Philanthropy. It defines the types of corporate giving by the level of benefit that accrues to the business, and is about the only way that the word charity is appropriate in this book's context.[i]

Charity
> Reactive community giving for which little or no business benefit is expected.

Community Investment
> Proactive grants that simultaneously aid long-term business goals and serve a critical community need.

Commercial
> Philanthropy in which benefit to the corporation is the primary motivation.

DISCONNECT #4 A FOCUS ON THE WRONG THINGS

There is an entire industry dedicated to procuring more dollars for the world's nonprofits. I am part of that industry and have been for many years. What has become apparent to me during my tenure is that the procurement activities overwhelmingly revolve around emotion rather than results. Emotions are, by definition, a part of the human condition and, in some ways, play a part in every decision a person makes, regardless of any conscious effort to keep them at bay for fear of making a less than optimal, wise, conscientious, (insert preferred word here) choice.

> *It seems that it has become more of a goal to get your money, rather than do good things with your money.*

That statement is likely to be unpopular and, truth be told, the altruistic side of me doesn't (want to) believe it. But working in the industry as I have, I can tell you that the statement has proven to be more true than false more times than I care to remember.

A few examples:

- Many times I have been in a client's office when that important grant is due, and everything else stops to focus all efforts on getting the application out the door.

- I have witnessed firsthand when more time and effort was spent discussing the message relayed by the picture on the cover of the annual report than by the content of the report itself.

- Almost anyone can tell you with which organization the ubiquitous pink ribbon is associated. This organization is a marketing master, and is so successful that in addition to the ribbons, we see flight attendants in pink shirts and even National Football League players with pink shoes. But the number of people who can tell me what they actually do, what outcomes they deliver, is much smaller.

DISCONNECT #5 PERCEIVED INEFFICIENCY

Investors, because they are approached constantly for donations, have developed an understandable aversion to the various fundraising pitches made by many nonprofits. Some of this stems from the fact that they cannot easily differentiate one nonprofit from another, neither by name nor outcomes.

As Nancy Lublin stated in her Ethonomics column in *Fast Company* magazine:

> "You can see it in the not-for-profit sector, which has a gazillion little organizations replicating one-another. We all want to run our own thing, so not-for-profits never die. As a result, we have huge inefficiency and ridiculous amount of overlap in the sector. This is wasteful, and this is fundamentally bad business."[ii]

Investors see perceived inefficiencies in many of the things their local nonprofits do, including:

- The annual black tie gala, held at the nicest place in town, which appears to cost more money than it raises.

- The endless number of golf tournaments and fun runs promoted by a host of local nonprofits, each approaching the usual suspects, of which investors almost always are, for sponsorships. Investors see their support of these events as not directly related to the outcomes they value, the outcomes that drew them to a particular organization in the first place.

- The annual appeals and/or membership dues for relatively small amounts of money. Investors usually participate, but then dislike the fact that they will undoubtedly be hit again for a much larger investment in an upcoming capital campaign.

While these inefficiencies may or may not be real, they do muddy the waters. They often have to be explained away, which gets in the way of why a given nonprofit deserves funding based on the outcomes it delivers.

DISCONNECT #6 MISUNDERSTANDING ROI

Traditionally, ROI in the fundraising world meant how much money was raised compared to how much money was spent on the effort. This, of course, is a very limited view and more along the lines of accounting methodology than the value of outcomes delivered.

The broader view of ROI is the total return to society, to the community, to the primary customers. This is closely related to what is termed SROI, or social return on investment, and is close to a true definition of what ROI means for an individual nonprofit. But even SROI has its limitations. Is this "social return" for a given financial investment or an attempt to put into financial terms what the consequences of a "social investment" might be? It is pursued from both perspectives, and there is no universal agreement on the conclusion.

ROI, by definition, is return divided by investment. The denominator is relatively easy to determine, depending on the context, such as:

- Expenditures over a given period of time;
- Expenditures for a given initiative/program;
- The amount of money raised in a campaign; or

- The amount given by a particular investor.

The numerator, on the other hand, is much more difficult to determine. Return is easy to measure when counting outputs or measures of activity, but more difficult when describing outcomes, which is the impact of the organization (or its mission) on the lives of its primary customers. It is because of this difficulty that many nonprofits remain stuck in describing ROI as how much money was raised at the event compared to the hard dollars it cost to produce. In that instance, it is an accounting term and nothing more. It does nothing to address the huge amounts of staff, volunteer, and board time spent on preparation, which does not show up on financial statements. It also misses the point: this has absolutely no relationship to the real return of what the organization delivers through its outcomes.

Many nonprofits are caught up in not truly understanding what ROI means to investors. For example, very few nonprofits have social events as part of their mission statement. Yet many, many nonprofits have social events every year. If you add up all the time spent by nonprofits on these events — field staff time, executive staff time, volunteer time, board member time, the disruption from delivering services, the planning, the opportunity costs — and you instead took that time and put it into the mission of the organization, the world truly would be a better place.

In other words, these events are done only for the purpose of raising money, but counterintuitively detract from why people give money to the nonprofit in the first place: their mission.

ROI in a fundraising context, as in the early stages of starting a campaign, normally begins with describing the broad social return for a given investment. This description frames the campaign and establishes broad community awareness. When it comes to an individual solicitation though, every attempt to get as specific as possible is crucial, meaning the specifics of a return for that individual investor. When we can answer the question "What's in it for me?" using a customized ROI approach, individual solicitations go well and campaigns meet or exceed goal.

REFERENCES

[i] "Giving in Numbers," *Committee Encouraging Corporate Philanthropy*, 2010 Edition, 41.
[ii] Nancy Lublin, "Let's hear it for the Little Guys," *Fast Company*, April 2010, 33.

Terms in This Chapter

Emotional Appeal

A fundraising technique designed to capitalize on a person's emotions in order to secure a donation.

Rational Appeal

A fundraising technique designed to involve a person's logical/deductive attributes in order to secure an investment in a nonprofit.

Value Proposition

The generic term that summarizes why someone should part with their assets, reasoning that the decision to do so will lead to more added value or better solve a problem than other similar offerings.

Financially Sustainable Organization

A nonprofit that consistently delivers outcomes that are valued by investors. Not to be confused with a self-supporting organization that generates enough earned income to continue operating.

Name-Brand Nonprofit

A large, national/international nonprofit commonly recognized because of highly visible, very costly advertising or marketing efforts.

CHAPTER 3

One Log Doesn't Make Much of a Fire

Give us your money or the panda gets it.
- *Attributed to George Smith*[i]

TWO SCHOOLS OF THOUGHT

In the war on what truly motivates people to give money, supporters of the emotional camp versus the rational camp appear diametrically opposed. The emotional camp is well-entrenched; the rational camp is relatively new in that it is finally gaining some traction in the broader nonprofit world after thriving in smaller circles for years. The fact that the two camps are viewed as almost mutually exclusive is also indicative of how entrenched the emotional traditionalists can be about their approach. If sustainable funding is analogous to a roaring fire, then many logs—including one or more emotional logs—is certainly necessary. Let's delve a little deeper into each camp before drawing comparisons.

THE EMOTIONAL CAMP

As long as nonprofit's have been in existence, emotional appeals have been the fundraising method of choice. Those who subscribe to its magic—also known as the psychic return—believe that people give for the warm glow they get in return. They also believe that "people give to people" and they spend lots of time—and money—figuring out the best way to tug at your heartstrings. Tom Ahern confirms this idea in his book, *Raising More Money With Newsletters Than You Ever Thought Possible*: "You already know that charity starts when you move a heart."[ii]

When deciding how strong one's allegiance should be to the emotional camp, every nonprofit needs to ask themselves questions like:

- Would I bet the organization on it?

- Would I bet the organization's ability to keep its doors open — to continue to fill a critical need — on it?

- Would I bet the organization's mission — its reason to exist — on it?

The "it" is the stubborn, traditional and increasingly ineffective school of thought that giving is purely, or largely, an emotional act. That one-log fire continues to put out less and less heat, and will eventually smolder itself out.

Emotional appeals range from the malnourished child staring directly at you from the cover of a glossy brochure to the direct appeal of a panhandler on the street, from the neighborhood kid selling popcorn door-to-door to the well-choreographed gala, complete with much cheering and peer pressure. They often contain personal stories meant to humanize the outcomes of the organization (which is a good thing) and anecdotal evidence designed to speak directly to the heart and trigger an emotion.

You don't need to look very far to see the next emotional appeal coming down the pike. On a given day I was:

- Awakened by the radio announcing the fun run this coming weekend;

- Saw abused pets, accompanied by Sarah McLachlan piano music, on a television commercial during the morning business news;

- Opened my mail to receive three solicitations for three different annual campaigns: an organization that helps children, one of my alma maters, and one of the large "name-brand" nonprofits;

- Received one call for a neighborhood clothing drive;

- Opened an e-mail, requesting I sponsor a runner for $5 a mile in the aforementioned fun run this weekend; and

- Spoke to a friend, inviting me to a black-tie gala for "only" $100 a seat.

You get the picture. And this was just an average day.

There's plenty of research, expert opinions, and real-world observations to back up the power of the emotional appeal. Some of the more interesting include:

Statistics get in the way

In the infamous Rokia study, a widely noted experiment with Save the Children, researchers found that donors who were given statistics about famine gave 25 percent more when also provided a photo of Rokia, a seven year old described as facing the "threat of severe hunger or even starvation." This follows common sense, since the picture humanizes the appeal. But what is more interesting is that they gave 66 percent more when given only general information and the photo. The study concluded that statistics "reduce empathy and interest in giving."[iii]

No information is better than good information

In the case of Child Fund International, donors gave more when told that the organization operated with "excellent efficiency" rather than "poor efficiency." And what happened when no information was offered about the organization's efficiency? This appeal received the highest response! According to Princeton psychology professor Danny Oppenheimer, "People give less when they are thinking analytically."[iv]

We want the warm glow... and then some

Economist James Andreoni argued in the 1980s that people really did give based on internal motives. In other words, they not only gave money to save the whales, ostensibly because they cared about whales, but also because they wanted to feel the "warm glow" that came from being viewed as the kind of person who would care enough to do something about saving the whales.[v] "Image motivation," the desire to be seen by others as a charitable person, has been used to describe this same phenomena.[vi]

We want to be like Warren

Similar to wanting to be viewed as the kind of person who is concerned about creatures of the deep, studies have shown some people give—in fact, sometimes considerably more than they initially intended—when they find out that someone they admire is also a giver to the organization or cause. When Warren Buffett gave $31 billion to the Gates Foundation, some experts speculated that the Foundation might run the risk of others not giving because they figured it now had all the money it needed. In actuality, even more money flowed in to the organization because many felt that Warren is a smart guy and savvy investor who must know a good cause when he sees it.[vii] In their minds, Mr. Buffett would never invest in an inefficient, ineffective nonprofit.

In still another example, donations at the Sierra Club increased 2.3 percent when told a major donor had made "a big contribution." John List, a highly respected behavioral economist who is known for taking a refreshing look at the sacred cows of traditional fundraising, offers that "people like to invest with a winner."[viii]

Sick beats healthy

A direct marketing company that consults with large, name-brand nonprofits has found that images of sick children outperform those of healthy ones in direct mail appeals. Their appeal letters create a sense of anxiety by describing a terrible problem, and then provide an easy solution: give money![ix]

We want to be winners

Real-world experience backs up the claim that more money flows when fundraising efforts are viewed as successful. This is why, in a capital campaign, a public kickoff is not announced until more than 50 percent of the goal is raised. It's also why we rarely see a United Way thermometer sign with only 10 percent "raised so far." These nuances make the goal—in effect, the cause—and the organization seem more legitimate.

Blondes have more fun... and raise more money

Researchers at East Carolina University found that when the door-to-door solicitor was an attractive female, donations doubled. To make it even more interesting, blondes raised 65 percent more than brunettes.[x]

To be fair, there are also emotionally based reasons why people don't give. Many of these reasons revolve around the concept of neutralization, which seeks to "soften or eliminate the effects on self-esteem and relationships with others when they act differently than expected [i.e. not giving]."[xi] Put another way, we neutralize when we don't want to feel badly about not giving money. Most of us would probably call this rationalization.

Some common examples of neutralization techniques are below:[xii]

1. Denial of responsibility: "I don't have enough money to give to charity. Other people — people with money — will take care of the need."

2. Denial of benefit: "I have been giving to the Cancer Society for years and they still haven't cured cancer."

3. Denial of victim: "If they would just get a job, they wouldn't be homeless."

4. Appeal to higher loyalties: "Charity begins at home. I need to look after my family first."

5. Endorsement backlash: "What right does that celebrity have to tell me what to do with my money?"[xiii]

To further refine the debate, it has been argued that people give for essentially two reasons: selfish motives or altruistic motives. People with selfish motives want something in return, while those with altruistic motives are rewarded through the communal relationships created by benefiting the organization.[xiv] This framing of the debate, put forth by Tom Farsides, a social psychology lecturer at the University of Sussex in England, is a natural transition to the other side of the argument: those motivated by rational motives.

THE RATIONAL CAMP

Rational appeals are the new kids on the block. Often synonymous with a more quantitative approach, they are usually portrayed as using cold, hard numbers and faceless facts. They are also identified more with left-brain activity, the side that deals with numbers, analytical thought, and logic as opposed to the right-brain activity usually associated with emotion, intuition, and creativity. Those in the emotional camp consider the use of numbers relatively ineffective. To quote Tom Ahern again, "They (numbers) can be surprisingly weak persuaders when you're trying to move people to give."[xv]

A columnist for the *Chronicle of Philanthropy*, the bible of the philanthropic world, once described the ROI-based, rational camp as "...a false dichotomy and one that threatens to undermine a movement that is sorely needed." The columnist further stated that "the Rokia study points to a real danger in the movement to encourage donors to give more rationally. While most everyone would like to see donors allocate their money based on a logical understanding of the problems they hope their gifts will solve, it turns out that encouraging donors to act this way may thwart their natural urge to give."[xvi]

Being in the fundraising business, why would I ever engage in anything that thwarts the natural urge to give? Such behavior would be counter-productive to my business. The Rokia study seems to be powerful evidence that people are irrational when it comes to making the decision to give, and how much to give, to nonprofits. So how do I dare to encourage people to follow me in refuting scholarly studies, done by renowned academics from Wharton and Carnegie Mellon?

The issue here is NOT that the studies are wrong; it's that they are studies. More precisely, studies that are too far removed from reality.

MOVING TO FIELD TRIALS

Empirical research can either be a statistical analysis of data or a controlled laboratory experiment. Academics will admit that laboratory experiments are done in an artificial environment; the next step in getting closer to the real world is a field trial. Field trials come nearer to reality by introducing aspects of real-world situations, usually by isolating one variable at a time so that valid conclusions can be reached.

The following summarizes three studies, all supporting the emotional camp, to underscore their limited usefulness in building a financially sustainable organization, which is what *Asking Rights* is all about.

1. A researcher wrote two different letters in an actual fundraising campaign. One letter said they had raised $2,000 towards a $3,000 goal. The other said they had raised $300 towards a $3,000 goal. The first letter proved to be much more effective.[xvii]

2. Another researcher circulated two stories describing the same situation. One told of a girl who was desperately poor and severely hungry, and that her chance at a better life was through the reader's donation. The other story described how food shortages are affecting more than three million children in one country, 11 million in another, and how in yet another country, one-third of the population had been forced to flee their homes. The first story was more likely to generate charitable donations.

3. Ordinary people in four experiments were given five $1 bills and presented with the opportunity to donate them all at once or piecemeal. Each experiment was designed to encourage "rational" thinking when making a decision about both identifiable and statistical victims. The conclusion was that people were most generous when asked to make a donation to an identifiable victim in the absence of "rational" analytic thought. In fact, the more statistical information people were given about a group of people, the less generous they became.

Now... on to the points that make these studies of limited use to capital campaigns in general, and to establishing *Asking Rights* in particular.

1. This study was conducted by John List, a University of Chicago economist and one of the most respected behavioral economists around. His conclusions were based on a written letter and his test amount was rather small.

2. This study was indeed the Rokia study. It was conducted by Deborah Small and two colleagues, leading researchers on how sympathy relates to charitable giving, and dealt with two versions of a story: one that humanized a victim, an "identifiable victim," versus one that presented both the "identifiable victim" and statistical victims. The most effective story contained scenarios of pain and suffering.

3. This study is also the Rokia study, presented differently and with more detail. The same methodology was used: five $1 bills and the choice to give that money based on several scenarios. One of the four experiments in the study included three possibilities: one with an identifiable victim, one with statistical victims, and one with an identifiable victim and statistical information. Another experiment actually primed analytic thinking. The stories were not necessarily related to the respondent; they were abstract.

What are the common threads that tie all these studies and conclusions together?

- Their experimental methodology often deals with impersonal channels, i.e. direct mail, letters, stories, random surveys, or phone calls from strangers.
- They deal with small amounts of money.
- They often use artificial circumstances not accurately reflective of everyday situations in which people are asked to give money.
- The subjects are often not personally connected to the cause.
- They only deal with individuals, not corporations or foundation boards/committees where funding decisions are commonly made by more than one person. Even in situations where individuals are asked for money, the actual decision often depends on others, such as a spouse or extended family members.

The Rokia studies approached people sitting alone in the student center of an Ivy League school.[xviii] At the risk of being politically incorrect, it's a huge risk for the average nonprofit to base their funding strategy on 20-somethings making decisions about trivial amounts of money just given to them.

The purpose of this discussion is not to pick apart the studies, but to illustrate how limited they can be in their application. I, as a practitioner in the fundraising/funding strategy business, cannot readily see how the action a person takes with $5 just given to him/her is at all similar to real-life situations dealing with how people choose to give their own hard-earned money. When designing an effective, sustainable funding strategy, it's important to base your strategies on the way people behave in actuality, not hypothetically.

I have heard many retellings of the Rokia study, to the point where the conclusion has become twisted: that numbers lead to less money raised. A sampling of the headlines from articles that refer to the Rokia study illustrates this perception:

- Heartstrings, Purse Strings;
- To Increase Charitable Donations, Appeal to the Heart - Not the Head; and
- Using Your Head and Your Heart in Philanthropy.

These titles do little to advance financial sustainability for nonprofits. They may apply to direct mail pieces, but a fundraising strategy is more than that, and developing *Asking Rights* is certainly a more complicated proposition. So while the studies themselves contain nuggets of useful information, it is difficult to envision using them as the basis for a fundraising strategy to build any sort of financially sustainable organization. The conclusions of these studies may help achieve a better response rate for direct mail efforts or raise a few more dollars for the annual campaign, but they have absolutely nothing to do with the outcomes delivered by the organization.

Just because you have honed your annual direct mail piece to a fine edge, it does not give you *Asking Rights*.

WHERE DOES THIS LEAVE US?

If you dig into the end notes in this chapter, you will see that the emotional camp studies are rigorous and academic. Many of the authors are economists and, sharing their appreciation for the impact of numbers, I applaud, subscribe to, and practice their approach. John List, the University of Chicago economist who clearly pitches his tent in the emotional camp, is ironically correct when he says, "I think most fundraisers are doing this wrong."[xix]

But I am also a realist. A classically trained economist would not be the best person to raise money for one of my clients. Even though a value proposition of Nobel Prize caliber will not raise money on its own, it is a great tool to help with that task. A great campaign case statement would not raise a dime if it were simply sent through the mail, but it is a necessary component of a successful capital campaign. And an experiment may make sense in the laboratory, but it loses some of its effectiveness in the real world.

Common sense and experience tells me many of the implications of the studies are correct. I, too, might give more money if not bombarded with statistics. I can also relate to an "identifiable victim" more readily than nameless, faceless statistics. And I would also probably give more money to an attractive woman than an unattractive one. But these facts together do not make the emotional camp triumphant or the rational camp incorrect. The choice is not mutually exclusive. While there is a place for the predominately emotional appeal, the rational appeal has been proven again and again to be more effective in certain funding situations.

What are these certain situations?

- When an organization is looking to become financially sustainable;
- When an organization wants to move beyond direct mail or impersonal channels for fundraising;
- When larger amounts of dollars are desired;
- When the outcomes delivered are valued by investors; and/or

- When the board/organization is more concerned with outcomes than appeals.

Some real-world context may make this more meaningful. When my company is raising money for our clients, our requests often make it to the boardroom. We want this to happen because the amount of money is usually more than an individual within the company has the ability to authorize on his/her own. When sitting in front of a dozen or so strangers, all with the right and, often, the predisposition to say "no" to anything that might require them to part with their money, I would much rather have rational, ROI-based ammunition than purely emotional bullets. If I'm going after big game, I want heavy caliber ammunition.

The situation described above raises some interesting questions that might point the way to research that has more practical applications.

Is the amount of money a determining factor?
There is some research that says it is.

How important is the channel of the ask?
Many existing studies involve direct mail or phone solicitations. Successful capital campaigns, however, where large amounts of money are involved, entail asks that are done in person.

How important is the relationship between the asker and the askee?
This is the darling of traditional fundraisers, possibly even more polarizing than the rational versus emotional debate. Traditionalists maintain that a personal relationship must exist. Yet large amounts of money are now raised by the most impersonal of channels — the web — and my company has raised hundreds of millions of dollars for clients through professional, in-person solicitations that are highly effective, even though we have no prior personal relationship with the investor.

Isn't anything that helps raise money for a nonprofit valuable?
From a rational perspective, there is no win in bettering your direct mail piece by using the same techniques as every other nonprofit. Imitation, in this instance, is not

flattery; it's a recipe for less than stellar results. How will potential supporters know it's your organization they want to support if your message sounds the same as the nonprofit down the block? What if all the time, effort, and money spent wordsmithing was spent on delivering outcomes that were valued by investors?

If raising money were only about emotional appeals, it should follow that the nonprofits that can craft the most gut-wrenching, heart-string-pulling, tear-jerking appeals will always raise the most money.

But that simply isn't the case.

The question remains: At the end of the day, does a nonprofit want to be known for its ad campaign or the results it delivers?

REFERENCES

[i] George Smith in *Up Smith Creek,* as quoted by Roger Craver (Sept. 28, 2011) "My Pantheon of Fundraising Curmudgeons," *TheAgitator.com*, Retrieved Sept. 28, 2011, from http://www.theagitator.net/dont-miss-these-posts/my-pantheon-of-fundraising-curmudgeons/

[ii] Tom Ahern, *Raising More Money With Newsletters Than You Ever Thought Possible* (Medfield: Emerson & Church, 2005), 15.

[iii] Anne Kadet, "Heartstrings, Purse Strings," *Smart Money*, December 2010, 100.

[iv] Ibid.

[v] David Leonhardt, "What Makes People Give?" *New York Times*, March 9, 2008.

[vi] Hans Eisenbeis (February 20, 2009). "Why do people give to charity? To look good," *Iconowatch.com*, Retrieved March 22, 2009, from http://blog.iconoculture.com/2009/02/20/why-do-people-give-to-charity-to-look-good/

[vii] Robert Smith (June 26, 2006). "Buffett Gift Sends $31 Billion to Gates Foundation," *NPR.com*, Retrieved Aug. 9, 2007, from http://www.npr.org/templates/story/story.php?storyId=5512893

[viii] Anne Kadet, "Heartstrings, Purse Strings," *Smart Money*, December 2010, 100.

[ix] Ibid.

[x] Ibid.

[xi] (July 25, 2005) "Why People Give (and do not give) To Charity," *AFP.net*, Retrieved April 3, 2008, from http://www.afpnet.org/Audiences/ReportsResearchDetail.cfm?ItemNumber=1544

[xii] Ibid.

[xiii] Ibid.

[xiv] Ibid.

[xv] Tom Ahern, *Raising More Money With Newsletters Than You Ever Thought Possible* (Medfield: Emerson & Church, 2005), 97.

[xvi] Sean Stannard-Stockton (Dec. 9, 2009), "Using Your Head & Your Heart in Philanthropy," *TacticalPhilanthropy.com*, Retrieved Oct. 25, 2011, from http://www.tacticalphilanthropy.com/2009/12/using-your-head-your-heart-in-philanthropy/

[xvii] David Leonhardt, "What Makes People Give?" *New York Times*, March 9, 2008.

xviii Deborah A. Small, George Loewenstein, and Paul Slovic, "Sympathy and callousness: The impact of deliberative thought on donations to identifiable and statistical victims," *Organizational Behaviors and Human Decision Processes 102,* March 3, 2006, 145.
xix David Leonhardt, "What Makes People Give?" *New York Times*, March 9, 2008.

Terms in This Chapter

Organizational Value Proposition®

An all-encompassing version of return on investment (ROI) specific to a nonprofit's outcomes. Introduced in the book *ROI for Nonprofits,* it is often abbreviated as OVP.

CHAPTER 4

Bus Drivers Eat Free

When asking for help, appeal to people's self-interest,
never to their mercy or gratitude.
- Robert Greene

MOTIVATIONS MATTER

In the 1970's, a popular billboard advertising campaign proclaiming "Bus Drivers Eat Free" was utilized by thousands of fast food restaurants, diners, and other establishments across the nation seeking the traffic of tour groups, school kids on field trips, and athletic teams. Although it isn't a widely employed sales tactic in today's day and age, back then, it had the power to entice an entire busload of people to a McDonald's for the price of a few hamburgers. The beauty of this promotion was two-fold.

1. It targeted exactly the right person, the decision-maker. The driver literally had control of the entire group. This was especially effective for the dining establishment that hosted those buses full of school children, where every passenger likely bought something. It was a sales phenomenon, one person was making the decision for 50 customers at one time.

2. It focused on the right motivations. The offer of free food by itself may have been motivation enough for the decision-maker to turn the bus towards the advertised location, but there was more to it. The bus driver was looking to keep his passengers happy. In the case of the school bus driver, it also made him the hero for stopping to get food for hungry kids, which made them more content and, often more quiet, passengers.

Targeting the call to action to the decision-maker is certainly important. But understanding the motivations of the decision maker is equally important. Right person, wrong message is no more effective than wrong person, right message. In Robert Greene's book, *The 48 Laws of Power*, Law #13 addresses this point by alluding to the fact that to get what you want, you must appeal to people's self-interest, not to their mercy.

There is much more to developing *Asking Rights* than just the discussion of emotional versus rational appeals, traditional views versus new approaches, and academic studies that may point to the wrong conclusion. One of the more important topics in the world of effective fundraising is motivations, which can vary widely and include different value propositions and different customer types.

TWO SEPARATE VALUE PROPOSITONS MAKE IT CONFUSING

I have often heard people oversimplify the idea that adopting a ROI-based approach is synonymous with running a nonprofit like a business. I'm really not sure what they mean when they say that. The literal meaning, that revenues must exceed expenses or the doors close, seems too simplistic. The conversation usually leads to people taking one of three positions.

1. It can't be done.
2. It shouldn't be done.
3. It has to be done.

Certainly the discipline of staying within budget, ensuring sound planning, satisfying customers, etc., are important to both for-profits and nonprofits. There is an obvious movement, though, to somehow make nonprofits more "business friendly," and it has birthed its own lexicon.

Philanthrocapitalism[i]
> Nonprofits should act more like businesses. Giving should be like investing. And capitalism should be more creative so long as it creates a wealth-class that gives back.

B Corporation
> A business model for entrepreneurs trying to create businesses with a social purpose.

Impact Investing
> Socially-responsible investing, seeking out commercial investments that return social good and profits.

Limited Liability Low Profit Company
> L3C, as it is called, is a legal form of organization (in some states) that combines for-profit efficiencies along with fewer regulations from the IRS to achieve socially beneficial goals. An L3C operates with a stated primary goal of achieving a social purpose, while making a profit is a secondary goal.

The vast and various array of differences between for-profits and nonprofits does not overshadow the valid points of both those who want to make them more similar and those who don't. But the only difference that really matters — in a fundraising context — is the value proposition that each delivers.

In the for-profit world, when an organization delivers value, it creates a source of revenue. For example, when I buy a new laptop, I receive value in the form of productivity, convenience, etc. The recipient of that value, me in this case, pays for that value. The maker of the computer, the producer/deliverer of that value, reaps revenue from my validation of that value. This dynamic creates a value proposition between the customer and the producer.

In the nonprofit world, there are typically two value propositions at work, the donor proposition and the beneficiary proposition.[ii] When a nonprofit delivers value to its primary customer, it has not found a source of revenue. Generally, the recipients of a service or product from a nonprofit do not pay for its value; someone else does that for them.

This same observation, in slightly different terms, was sent my way by Brigid Slipka, Director of the Annual Giving Program at California Institute of the Arts, in reaction to my guest post on TacticalPhilanthropy.com in December 2010. My original post — submitted with the title *In Defense of ROI* but renamed *Impact*

Focused Fundraising on the blog—was in response to the emotional appeal argument previously discussed in Chapter 3.

First, my original post.

Impact Focused Fundraising
By Tom Ralser

I love academic studies. I love some old-school ways of doing things. What I love the most is what works.

When I sent Sean a copy of *The Traditional Fundraisers Coloring Book,* a tongue-in-cheek look at how most fundraisers conduct capital campaigns, he replied that although he is certainly in favor of a more rational approach for funding to flow to deserving nonprofits, he respected the evidence that supported the contrary view that "donors react best to emotional pitches."

I understand that emotional appeals work, and they have been honed to a fine edge by fundraisers for years. There is an entire industry built around it, complete with its own dogma, trade associations, and publications. To be completely honest, I have never seen a dollar raised because of numbers on a page. When given the choice between a page of statistics and a picture of a starving child staring you in the face, the emotional appeal will win almost every time. To have a real discussion about this, though, we need to move beyond a one dimensional and mutually exclusive playing field.

When I get requests for an Organizational Value Proposition®, an ROI analysis, or some other version of quantitative crunching from a nonprofit, my first question is "What do you hope to do with it?" No matter how good or compelling the analysis, unless effective communication and sound fundraising techniques are used in conjunction with these magical numbers, they do no good. Conversely, a solely emotional appeal also has its limitations, namely that they are less effective than they used to be, often result in lower investment amounts, and do not do well in corporate "asks."

The best toolbox contains both emotional and ROI/outcome-based approaches. Being in the funding business, I prefer to hit on all cylinders, or to use another cliché, use the right tool for the right job. Often the emotional connection is the entrée to the "ask," but the justification for larger dollars is accomplished by a more rational value proposition.

In the Rokia study mentioned by Sean, the fact that a statistical ingredient (distraction may be a better word) led to less giving is not at all surprising. Although somewhat antiseptic and not reflective of a real world fundraising situation (they were giving away $5 or less of newly received money, they did not have a connection with the cause to begin with, they were not approached by a professional with a strong value proposition in hand, only general statistics were presented, etc.), I am sure it is a very fine clinical study. It's the translation of that study into a real world, in the trenches fundraising situation where the conclusions of that study wear thin. Give me those same subjects and realistic conditions in a true fundraising situation, and I can almost guarantee I will be able to get larger investments with a non-emotional appeal.

An analogy may help frame the debate. Buying an automobile is often considered an emotional event, and one that Madison Avenue has spent much time refining. Some people will buy for the image portrayed in the commercials. Some will buy for the color. Some will buy because it is "cute." Some will even buy for the smell. There is a large segment, though, that buys for the numbers: horsepower, zero to 60 times, and miles per gallon. These are cold, hard, non-emotional numbers that often make the difference between parting with your money or not... just like fundraising.

For a real-time fundraising example, this month we will be finishing a campaign for a local chapter of a national youth organization. We went over 40 percent over goal in an eleven month campaign, raising almost $2 million. The campaign was based entirely on a value proposition/ROI approach. Did we have pictures of children in our campaign collateral? Yes. Is this what got several $200,000 plus investments? No. Every one of the dozen or so campaigns we are now engaged in uses an ROI approach, some almost exclusively.

I think the discussion may be more instructive if it heads toward *what* numbers are used, how they are related to the specific prospect, and how close they dare to tread toward the "What's in it for me?" end of the spectrum. At the end of the day, when I am charged with raising several million dollars in 12 months or less, I am going to use the most effective means available, and an outcome-based approach is the hands down choice.

Now her well-crafted response.

When Apple pitched the iPhone to shareholders, it went into the details. Steve Jobs talked for hours, statistics were distributed, supply chain was analyzed, P&L statements discussed.

When Apple pitched the iPhone to customers, it did this:

(link to video clip for iPhone)

There is a difference between an investor in a company and a buyer of the company's product. The investor has a desire to see the company succeed on a broad scale across the market. The customer wants the company to succeed in bringing that individual product to her.

Same is true in nonprofit fundraising. Some donors are invested. They want proof of long term-results & impact on communities

And some donors just want the happy rush from an act of goodwill.

There's nothing inherently better about an investor-donor versus a customer-donor. Investors are prevalent at the early stages of a nonprofit's lifecycle, but eventually the customer-donors must be in place for a mature organization to build stability into its future revenues.

The potential problems come in mixing up the two. As with the iPhone, investors and buyers need different types of pitches and different types of communication. Investors are focused on the information that can be delivered from a spreadsheet; buyers choose to give from information delivered from an emotive story. If you give investors an emotive story, they will roll their eyes and not give. If you give customers spreadsheets, they will click away and also not give.

On Sean's website at Tactical Philanthropy, Tom Ralser wrote about the ways to communicate through ROI (Return on Investment, i.e. investor-donor stuff) versus emotional storytelling (i.e. buyer-donor stuff). He writes that the ROI wins in the most-effective-fundraising category, hands-down:

A solely emotional appeal also has its limitations, namely that they are less effective than they used to be, often result in lower investment amounts, and do not do well in corporate "asks." …I can almost guarantee I will be able to get larger investments with a non-emotional appeal.

What I see missing, however, is that the donors Ralser is targeting are not your givers of $25 or $100, but of an investment that requires a deeper analysis of impact among an entire population. To appeal to a donor who has a quicker interaction with a nonprofit–a fast text donation or online gift–an emotive fundraising story is required instead.

Which brings us to GiveWell, which has been touting the amazing impacts of their very best-rated nonprofit, VillageReach, in terms that appeal to investor-donors. A few days ago they wrote about the need to appeal to buyer-donors as well. So they are asking for fundraising pitches that focus not on the spreadsheet-driven information, but the emotional stories that appeal to buyer-donors.

I plan to throw out a few suggestions (and if you'd like to do so, you can submit your comments here). The challenge will be in the tension between the GiveWell audience, which focuses on numeric results, versus the general giving population, who are swayed by emotional stories.

Ultimately, the argument that is most persuasive will depend on which audience we want to reach.

I cannot argue with her conclusion; it depends. There are several subtle points, though, that merit a closer look.

1. Ms. Slipka seems to be looking at my use of the word "investor" through a for-profit lens. Investors are not limited to the early stages of a nonprofit. I use the term to imply a focus on outcomes, which are important at any stage.

2. Ms. Slipka implies that an investor (investor-donor) is synonymous with a large amount of money and a customer (customer-donor) is synonymous with a small amount, referencing $25 and $100 amounts. I will go as far to say that the larger the amount of money, the more serious the discussion might become, but I will not correlate the amount of money being discussed with prospects with the level of outcomes they desire. The term "investor" has more to do with the fact that a person giving money wants to see a valuable outcome delivered rather than an absolute financial level.

At this point, if we combine these thoughts, we are left with an almost three-dimensional situation consisting of the donor proposition, which can be split into two further categories of investor-donor and customer-donor, and the beneficiary proposition, which encompasses the receiver of the services. Yes, this can get confusing.

Another way to approach this topic is by framing it in terms of customers. As first put forth by Peter Drucker, nonprofits have primary customers and supporting customers. Primary customers are those whose lives are changed by the nonprofit's efforts and are directly related to the beneficiary value proposition discussed earlier. Supporting customers — staff, volunteers, board members and especially funders — are those who choose to participate in making the nonprofit's efforts possible, with the overarching goal of helping to make the organization successful in its mission. They are directly related to the donor value proposition.

Yet a fourth way of describing the differing attributes of nonprofit funders/supporting customers has recently emerged: impact buyers. Jason Saul introduces this term, claiming there are people who "attach real value to key social outcomes and make rational decisions to 'purchase impact.' These stakeholders focus more on value than values."[iii] Having dealt with people who would certainly fit into this category throughout my career, there is an immediate, but not complete, agreement with this description of how some investors make decisions. In fact, there is enough agreement that it deserves to be discussed in more depth in subsequent chapters. But for now, let's leave it as another way to describe the complicated relationships of motivations, value propositions, and different strokes for different folks.

Whether the term is donor value proposition/beneficiary value proposition, investor-donor/customer-donor, or primary customer/supporting customer, they all describe the complex funding world where nonprofits dwell. Naturally, with two vastly different types of customers running around demanding two completely different value propositions and potentially two different types of investors within one category — and no universal agreement on any of the above — reaching a conclusion can be difficult. It's like the old joke about the academic nature of economists: If you took all of the economists in the world and laid them end to end, they still would not reach a conclusion.

THE INVESTOR MOTIVATION MATRIX

Introducing yet another dimension to this discussion may at first appear to make it more confusing, but I believe it may actually make it more meaningful. The relationship between a funder's motivations and his or her level of financial involvement, with the addition of the activities or programs to be funded, can make the discussion more productive, no matter what label (donor, investor, beneficiary, customer, impact buyer, etc.) is used.

At its simplest level, the Investor Motivation Matrix shown in Exhibit 4.1 is built on two axes: financial commitment and motivation/appeal. The vertical (Y) axis represents the motivation/appeal used to secure funding for a given program and ranges from purely emotional appeals to purely rational appeals. In this discussion, appeals and motivations can be used synonymously. The horizontal axis (X) represents the funder and ranges from the donor that represents a small financial commitment to an investor who represents a large financial commitment.

Exhibit 4.1 Basic Investor Motivation Matrix

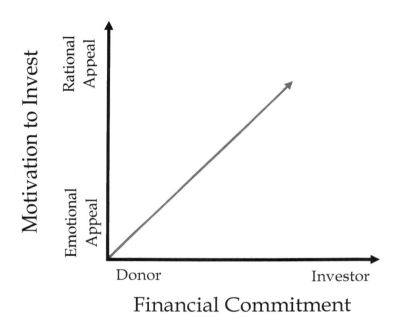

In a simplistic world, this line would be a linear function where motivation is directly related to financial commitment. The world of fundraising, however, is not that simple and motivations can be complex and subject to wide variations, as can financial capacity and ability. What is most useful if plotted on these axes is a representation of the activity/service/program being funded, categorized by some general attributes. An honest inventory of an organization's programs based on the appeal/motivation and the amount of investment involved can yield an interesting financial profile. Not a profile based on stale, internally focused financially ratios, but one much more important and externally focused: what motivations allow these programs to be funded and to what level.

Note: As I have said before, I prefer not to use the term "donor" since it implies a charity mindset. However, to be consistent with the donor value proposition discussion earlier in this chapter, I will use it here for illustrative purposes.

If we divide the plot area into four quadrants, there are four distinct types of efforts, as you can see in Exhibit 4.2.

Exhibit 4.2 Investor Motivation Matrix Quadrants

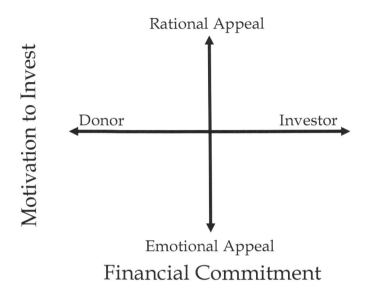

Obviously, there are no finite boundaries between the quadrants. There is no definitive level of financial commitment, for example, that distinguishes a donor and his/her respective donation from an investor and his/her respective investment. The moving from a purely emotional appeal, for example, to a rational appeal can incorporate an increasingly more rational flavor, until the majority of the appeal becomes more rational than emotional.

FOUR ACTIVITY/PRODUCT CATEGORIES

The four quadrants delineated by these axes lead to a guide for categorizing activities or programs for which funding is being sought. These categories of Heart, Acorn, Shooting Star, and Blue

Chip are pictured in Exhibit 4.3, and are easy ways to relate the need, the motivation, and the funder in one, unified graphic image.

Exhibit 4.3 Investor Motivation Matrix Categories

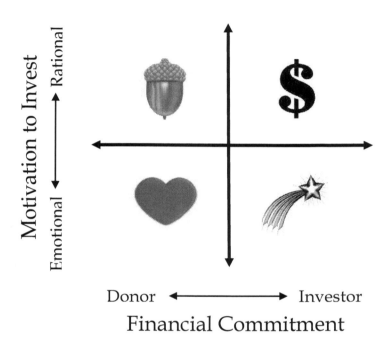

Heart
Financial Involvement: Low
Appeal: Emotional

We see these types of appeals all of the time. These are activities or programs that depend on lots of smaller donations, which are secured by emotional appeals that tug on the heartstrings.

Example: A countertop collection for an animal shelter, where abused pets are brought back to health and then adopted into a good home.

Acorn
Financial Involvement: Low
Appeal: Rational

These are activities or programs that depend on relatively smaller amounts of dollars, but where a rational appeal is more effective. Acorns can grow; they have the potential to mature into Blue Chip programs.

Example: A membership drive for the operation of a local Chamber of Commerce, where membership dues are based on the size of the company and where membership carries with it certain privileges or benefits.

Shooting Star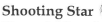
Financial Involvement: High
Appeal: Emotional

These efforts are the superstars that grab all of the headlines and raise lots of money. They are activities or programs that are highly visible and the need is considered obvious or necessary, which leads to large amounts of money being raised through emotional appeals.

Example: A one-time campaign for a hospital emergency room that needs refurbishing and updating, made obvious by a tragedy in which lives were lost due to lack of modern equipment.

Blue Chip $
Financial Involvement: High
Appeal: Rational

These are activities or programs that require larger amounts of funding and evidence of effectiveness, results, or valuable outcomes will be required to secure that funding.

Example: A capital campaign for an economic development program that will create jobs, increase capital investment, and produce positive, long-term economic ripple effects.

Using this matrix to graphically represent where the programs in need of funding fall can be eye opening, and its usefulness in developing *Asking Rights* can be powerful. For example, if an organization finds that its programs are funded by emotional appeals and many but small donations, then there is certainly an opportunity to develop a more rational appeal focused on larger, sustainable investments. In the case where a few high profile programs generate lots of funding but are relying solely on emotional appeals (the Shooting Stars), an effort towards more rational appeals will be more sustainable, since Shooting Stars tend to burn brightly but then burn out.

Asking Rights can be most fully developed on the upper half of the chart (Acorns and Blue Chips) since they place such a high importance on outcomes, which tend to gain traction quickly with the more rational motivations of investors. Strategies that actively work to move programs in the direction of more rational motivations and therefore larger investments (Hearts to Acorns to Blue Chips, or Hearts to Shooting Stars to Blue Chips) are those that can benefit the most from developing *Asking Rights*.

REFERENCES

[i] Lucy Bernholz, "Philanthropy's 10 Favorite Buzzwords of the Decade Show How Nonprofits are Changing," *The Chronicle of Philanthropy*, January 3, 2011.
[ii] William Landes Foster, Barbara Christianses and Kim Peter, "Ten Nonprofit Funding Models," *Stanford Social Innovation Review,* Spring 2010.
[iii] Jason Saul, *The End of Fundraising* (San Francisco: Jossey-Bass, 2001), 87.

CHAPTER 5

Why People Give

Nobody but a beggar chooses to depend chiefly upon the benevolence of his fellow citizens.
- Adam Smith

WHY PEOPLE GIVE: CONVENTIONAL WISDOM

Why do people give? Ahh, the million-dollar question. Actually, it's a $298 billion question, according to the amount of money American's gave in 2012.[i] Type the phrase "Why do people give" into a Google search and you are likely to get more than two billion results.

Even though this question has been studied for years, most of the attempts to answer it are, as expected, fairly predictable. There are far too many studies, articles, and opinions to list them all. Four examples that are easy to digest and representative of the lot are presented below.

Example 1
Timothy Burgess, "Why People Give."[ii]

1. Anger
2. Ego Gratification
3. Exclusivity
4. Fear
5. Greed
6. Guilt

Example 2
Shai Davis, "9 Reasons People Give Charity, and 1 More."[iii]

1. Hope
2. Association
3. Friends
4. Sadness
5. Make a Difference
6. Love
7. Dreams
8. Faith
9. The consulting firm which placed the ad
10. Guilt

Example 3
Rebecca Ruby and Katya Andresen, "The Secret to Getting People to Give: 15 Reasons Why People Donate."[iv]

1. Someone I know asked me to give, and I want to help them.
2. I felt emotionally moved.
3. I want to feel I'm not powerless in the face of need and can help.
4. I want to feel I'm changing someone's life.
5. I feel a sense of closeness to a community or group.
6. I need a tax deduction.
7. I want to memorialize someone.
8. I was raised to give to charity - it's a tradition.
9. I want to be "hip" and this charity is popular.
10. It makes me feel connected to others.
11. I want to have a good image for myself or my company.
12. I want to leave a legacy that perpetuates me, my ideals, or my cause.

13. I feel fortunate (or guilty) and want to give something back.

14. I give for religious reasons.

15. I want to be seen as a leader/role model.

Example 4
Jerold Panas, "People Give Because…"[v]

1. They believe in the work of your organization and its unique qualifications to provide the program and services you propose.

2. They are persuaded their gift will change lives or save lives.

3. They have the money to give. Without appropriate financial capacity, there can be no gift.

4. They understand that because of the investment, they'll make an impact of lasting value.

5. There is philanthropic intent. Regardless of net worth or annual income, if there isn't philanthropic intent, there probably won't be a gift.

6. They will be joining others in a worthy cause. Donors like to know they're not alone, that others are joining the program. Everyone enjoys being a part of the bandwagon effect.

7. You *ask* them to make an investment. It's amazing what you don't raise when you don't ask.

As you can see, there is much agreement and many reasons that overlap. While the word "altruism" seems glaringly absent, the meaning of the word is reflected in such phrases as "making a difference." The premise of the rational camp does occasionally peek through, even if subtly. References to exclusivity (Example 1, #5), a financial gain (Example 3, #6), and self-interest (Example 2, #2; Example 3, #s 3,4,5,9,10,12 and 13; Example 4, #6) all denote some form of rational motivation. Even the examples that describe how a person feels do not necessarily equate to a purely emotional reason. For example, I may want to feel close to a community or group out of an emotional need for belonging or I may want to be close to a group for purely selfish reasons. The more extreme form of self-interest — "What's in it for me?" — shows up in Example 3, #s 11 and 15.

The last list in particular deserves the most consideration because it came from Jerold Panas, one of the more well-known veterans of fundraising. Notice, though, that he uses the word "gift" and "investment" almost interchangeably, which is where he and I diverge. I feel strongly that they are diametrically opposed.

Next are some additional thoughts on why people give that have shown up in some of the strangest places but apply directly to fundraising.

On Self-Interest

"People aren't going to make decisions just to save the earth. But if you can save $1,000 a year, you're going to change your behavior." This appeared in an article about paying for car insurance by the mile. Recent studies by the Brookings Institution and The University of California, Berkeley, found that paying for insurance by the mile would reduce miles driven by 8 percent.[vi] Even though a person might not really care about driving less to emit less carbon dioxide and have less negative impact on the planet, their self-interest in saving money creates the by-product of social good.

On Behavioral Economics and Neuroeconomics

Dr. Paul Zak, aka Dr. Love, has studied the link between empathy and generosity and their relationship to oxytocin, a chemical that acts as an "economic lubricant." Whereas Dan Ariely, author of *Predictably Irrational*, and Stephen Levitt, co-author of *Freakonomics*, are famous for studying how economic decisions are made, Dr. Zak is more concerned with why they are made. His conclusions are not final, but his first study in 2010 indicated that people given oxytocin donated an average of 48 percent more to charity than those given a placebo.[vii] This is important in that this was the first time the study was expanded to include giving money to organizations, not just individuals.

On Exclusivity

A study of donors who made gifts to 10 cultural institutions in Pittsburgh found that those who gave the most were wealthy individuals who had been invited to exclusive, high-profile events. "Individuals with high levels of wealth ... place a much higher value on the private benefits associated with their giving."[viii]

On Demographics

Older people equate happiness with peacefulness, while younger people equate happiness with excitement, according to a study of 2,600 blogs that looked for ways in which people described what made them happy.[ix] From a fundraising perspective, collateral pieces that are designed to promote vibrant, current, ever-changing messages will not work very well on the over 50 crowd who, by the way, have more money and are more willing to part with it in the name of nonprofits.

On Corporate Giving

Even though the United States leads the world in corporate giving, it has "little to do with the spirit of charitable giving," as reported in Inc. magazine.[x] When presented with a list of reasons to engage in corporate social responsibility, American corporations were the least likely to cite the motivation of "saving the earth." Overall, this type of idealism was given by only 21 percent of U.S. corporations as compared to 40 percent of non-U.S. companies.

Overall, these articles, lists, and studies are in general agreement, and the vast majority are based on emotional reasons (with the few exceptions being those darned business people and naturally occurring chemicals).

WHY DO YOU GIVE: A PRIMARY EXPERIMENT

You can see at this point why it is difficult to move the ball forward for the rational appeal camp. So much of the existing material is firmly rooted in the emotional, traditional camp. Since I am often in front of groups giving presentations or facilitating workshops, I thought I would simply ask people: "Why Do You Give?"

To set the stage with my audience, I typically hand out a series of questions at the beginning of our time together. Since my primary professional focus is on nonprofits, many of the attendees are tied to that world in one way or another. Some are nonprofit executive directors, some are senior staff. Many are board members.

So, is the sample somewhat self-selective? Yes, but in a good way; these board members are normally the leaders in their respective communities, so they are asked — often and repeatedly — for money by a wide range of nonprofits. Does being employed by a nonprofit make one predisposed to giving money? Maybe. Do those same people have less money to give, since nonprofits are not the highest paying industries? Yes. These factors, though, point to responses that lend themselves to be more conservative and well thought through than the population in general.

Before you read on, I invite you to take the quiz yourself and record your answers for reference as the results are discussed. If you could also take a moment to email your answers to **whydoyougive@convergentnonprofit.com**, I would greatly appreciate it, as I discuss the results of this quiz frequently in my various speaking engagements and am always looking to increase my data pool.

Why Do You Give?
Please circle one response per question

1. When are you most likely to give?

   A. When asked in person
   B. When asked by telephone
   C. When asked by mail
   D. When asked by email
   E. When asked by social media

2. When asked in person to give, in which situation are you most likely to give?

   A. When someone you know asks you to give
   B. When someone you do not know personally, but representing a nonprofit that you **are** familiar with, asks you to give
   C. When someone that you do not know personally, representing a nonprofit that you **are not** familiar with, asks you to give

3. Which of the following is most likely to cause you to invest in a nonprofit?

   A. A hand-written letter from an acquaintance (not a personal friend)
   B. A form with predetermined financial levels that you can check
   C. A note with a small gift (value under $5)
   D. A brochure with a picture of a person in need looking directly at you

4. Which of the following is most likely to cause you to invest $25 in a nonprofit?

   A. A cause with which you identify
   B. Being asked by someone you know

5. Which of the following is most likely to cause you to invest $500 in a nonprofit?

   A. A cause with which you identify
   B. Being asked by someone you know

6. Which of the following is most likely to cause you to invest in a nonprofit?

   A. A nonprofit that you identify with, but are **not sure** they are delivering valuable results
   B. A nonprofit that you **do not** identify with, but are confident they are delivering valuable results

The results below are actual tabulations from eight audience groups scattered throughout the country and across different economic sector types, including a Southern community foundation board; a local chapter of a national, professional fundraising association located in a wealthy Northeast area; the staff of a Southern regional arts and culture organization; a workshop for area nonprofit executives in the high tech, wealthy area near Stanford University; a community foundation workshop series for nonprofit executives in the Midwest; a human services board in the West; executives of an international educational institution on the East Coast; and community leaders of a civic organization in the South.

In total, 102 responses were tallied and the responses were very lopsided. While the sample size may not be large enough for a 95 percent confidence level or +/- 2 percent in precision, the results do shed some light on actual behavior based on primary research. The results, by question, can be summarized as follows:

1. Eighty percent said they are most likely to give when asked in person.

2. Seventy-three percent said they are most likely to give when they know the person asking, 26 percent when they know the organization.

3. Sixty-two percent said that when not being asked to give in person, a hand-written note is the next best thing.

4. Sixty percent said the cause is more important than the person asking if the amount is relatively small.

5. Fifty-nine percent said the cause is more important than the person asking if the amount is 20 times higher.

6. Seventy-three percent said that the results being delivered are more important than the cause if results are dubious or uncertain.

In general, one can draw three conclusions:

1. Personal interaction is important, as is knowing the person doing the asking;

2. Causes are <u>more</u> important than knowing the person doing the asking, even when the amount of money is 20 times higher; and

3. Results matter.

A closer examination reveals even more insight. The first question was not why they give, but how they respond to various methods of asks. The top answer supports one of the most often repeated axioms of traditional fundraising: "people give to people." In fact, it was emailed to me on July 16, 2012, as the main theme of Monday Morning Matters, the weekly email from *AskingMatters.com*.[xi]

The next most popular response was by mail. Social media got two responses. Do the responses surprise me? Quite frankly, with these groups it did since many of these respondents received a major portion of their annual funding from annual campaigns, which were done by mail. In general, though, the answer fits with what successful fundraisers have known for a long time, which is why I always advocate in-person asks.

The second question delves deeper into the in-person issue, and it was no surprise that the first two answers received 99 percent of the responses. With 73 percent saying that when asked in-person they are "most likely" to give when they know the person and another 26 percent saying they are "most likely" to give when they know the organization being represented, it's safe to say that some degree of familiarity is important.

The third question has to do with the form of a non-personal appeal and had the most disparate answers of any question. Notes with small gifts received only two responses. The person in need staring right at you from a brochure cover received only 10 percent of the responses. (Take that, Rokia!) A preprinted form with predetermined levels of giving got an unexpected 26 percent. This is consistent with the fact that many of the organizations received much of their funding from annual campaigns, which notoriously employs this method, but is not consistent with how the first question was answered. Is it surprising that a hand-written note received the highest response at 62 percent? Not at all, the personal touch is still very powerful.

Now, the interesting part. The fourth question was a forced choice between a cause and the solicitation, with everything being stacked in the favor of the solicitation: being asked by someone they know. The amount was kept relatively low at $25. Remember, the first question already told us that 80 percent give when asked in person and the second question told us that 73 percent are "most likely" to give when they know the person. Despite the previous answers, 60 percent said that a cause with which they could identify trumped being asked by a person they know.

The fifth question was the very same question, only the amount was bumped up to $500, 20 times the original amount. The results did not measurably change, with 59 percent still responding that the cause was more likely to trigger them to part with their money. In aggregate, the amount of money in question does not change the answer when forced to choose between a cause and who is doing the asking. I had surmised, based on personal experience, that as the amount of money in question went up, the type of solicitation, i.e. the person doing the asking, would become more important. These results do not support that. The discussion that ensued among the participants taking the quiz, though, often cited the amounts of money as the reason for their answers. This suggests that had I used an even larger amount, say $1,000 instead of $500, then their responses would have been different.

A blanket statement of "cause is always more important than a personal relationship in fundraising" would also not be true. It does point to the fact that a personal relationship is not always a prerequisite for successful fundraising. This is not inconsistent with the results of the first and second questions; it just introduces a completely new dimension into the old fundraising argument that "people give to people." Yes, they prefer to give to people, but what they are giving money to is often even more important than the channel or method of the solicitation.

Not satisfied with the above results, I dug deeper into these two questions. Remember, the only thing that changed between the fourth and fifth questions was the amount of money involved, $25 or $500 respectively. Fifty-six percent did not change their minds between the two questions. Of those that did change their responses, 23 respondents went from cause to person and 22 respondents went from person to cause as the amount of money in question went up.

How do we make sense of these unexpected results? While six out of 10 people are motivated to give more by the cause than the person, two of those six are likely to place more importance on the person asking as the amount of money goes up. On the other hand, while four out of 10 people are motivated more by the person asking than the cause, two of those four are more likely to place more importance on the cause as the amount of money goes up.

The results of the last question got to the heart of the matter. Again, it is a forced choice, but instead of choosing between a cause and who is asking, this time the choice is between identifying with a cause/organization and the results they deliver, with no amount of money specified. When given the choice of cause or results, they overwhelmingly chose results: 73 percent to 27 percent. These respondents, like most people, do not want their money wasted.

Do these results fit in nicely with my point of view of rational appeals and outcomes mattering the most? Yes, yes they do. Was the quiz rigged to produce these results? Absolutely not. To the contrary, I expected different results. I thought I would see that for relatively small amounts of money, such as $25 in the fourth question, the cause would be more important. I thought in the fifth question that the $500 amount would cause answers to be reversed, since they would rely on the credibility of the person they knew to part with their dollars.

The last question, though, could have been easily biased by saying that you are "suspect" that the organization is delivering valuable results. Or that the results themselves were "dubious in nature." I chose the least biasing words I could find: "not sure." Did the groups involved in the quiz, by nature of their association with the nonprofit industry in one way or another, bias the answers so strongly in favor of results? Possibly. At the end of the day, though, was it gratifying to see that results matter? You bet it was.

One study that directly reinforces the position that outcomes matter is a 2012 study produced by Cygnus Applied Research. This study involved the responses of more than 15,000 donors (real people who give real money) to a wide range of charitable causes.[xii] As reported in the *Chronicle of Philanthropy,* "Donors... want to support organizations that achieve strong results." More precisely, middle-aged donors "want to be offered a clear idea of where their money is going," and "want to know that the charity is the best of all organizations working on that mission."[xiii] Sounds like an Organizational Value Proposition® (hereinafter referred to as "Organizational Value Proposition" or "OVP" without the registered trademark symbol used to facilitate readability) to me.

A SUMMARY... MAYBE

As I have stated before, I am a big fan of what works in the real world. Rational appeals work in many situations, but if I am charged with raising money, I am going to use the best tool or tools available. Let me give a real-world example of how completely different approaches can work well on the same project. In this example, a rural hospital is in need of upgrades to both infrastructure and equipment.

To the retired grandparent:
The hospital needs a new emergency room and all of the expensive equipment that goes with it. We need to reconfigure the parking lot and access so that those going to the emergency room can save valuable minutes. When your granddaughter gets a compound fracture in her leg during soccer practice, you don't want to have to drive 45 minutes to the next county for quality emergent care. We need this now.

To the major employer:
Not having a modern emergency room reflects badly on the community. It could negatively impact your ability to attract talent, especially younger workers with families. Economic growth in the area will likely suffer without this important community asset. In fact, access to quality healthcare is at the top of the list of what people look for when choosing a community in which to put down roots. All of these combine to negatively impact your future labor pool. We need this now.

In the first example, it was an appeal based entirely on fear, a purely emotional appeal. In the second, it was an appeal based on "What's in it for me?", a purely rational appeal. Both have their place.

REFERENCES

[i] Giving USA Foundation, "The Annual Report on Philanthropy 2011, Executive Summary," (Chicago: Giving USA Foundation, 2012): 4.

[ii] Timothy Burgess (Jan. 16, 2007). "Why People Give," *FundRaising Success*, Retrieved April 3, 2008, from http://www.fundraisingsuccessmag.com/article/why-people-give-45500/1#

[iii] Shai Davis (June 14, 2007). "9 Reasons People Give Charity, and 1 More," *Fundraising Seeds*, Retrieved April 3, 2008 from http://www.fundraisingseeds.com/?p=32&print=1

[iv] Rebecca Ruby and Katya Andresen (March 6, 2008). "The Secret to Getting People to Give: 15 Reasons Why People Donate," *Network for Good Learning Center*, Retrieved April 3, 2008 from http://www.fundraising123.org/print/312

[v] Jerold Panas, "People Give Because…" *Contributions Magazine, Vol. 26 No.2,* June 2012.

[vi] Cliff Kuang, "Insurance by the Mile," *FastCompany*, April 2010, 32.

[vii] Adam Penenberg, "Doctor Love," *FastCompany,* July/August 2010, 80.

[viii] Holly Hall, "Proving What Works in Fundraising: Scholars Dispel Myths," *The Chronicle of Philanthropy*, August 25, 2009.

[ix] Jeff Brooks (Aug. 12, 2010) "What donors want from life – it's likely not what you want," *Future Fundraising Now,* Retrieved Aug. 15, 2010, from http://www.futurefundraisingnow.com/future-fundraising/2010/08/what-donors-want-from-life-its-likely-not-what-you-want.html

[x] Mike Hofman, "The Best Cause of All," *Inc.*, June 2008, 23.

[xi] Asking Matters, "Monday Morning Matters" weekly member email, July 16, 2012.

[xii] Penelope Burke, The Cygnus Donor Survey: Where Philanthropy is headed in 2012 (Chicago: Cygnus Applied Research, June 2012) 41.

[xiii] Raymund Flandez, (June 21, 2012) "Donors Say They Would Give More If They Saw More Results," *The Chronicle of Philanthropy,* Retrieved on June 21, 2012 from http://philanthropy.com/article/Many-Donors-Would-Give-More-if/132437/

Terms in This Chapter

Form 990
An annual informational return required of many nonprofits. Similar to a for-profit tax return, but with no tax consequences, it contains basic information on revenues, expenses, assets, liabilities, executive compensation, and board makeup.

GuideStar
"The nonprofit industry's leading resource for nonprofit data."[i]

Charity Navigator
"America's largest and most influential charity rater."[ii]

GiveWell
"...a nonprofit dedicated to finding outstanding giving opportunities and publishing the full details of our analysis to help donors decide where to give."[iii]

Bayesian Prior
Prior beliefs and how they are updated using Bayes Theorem, which describes the relationship between evidence, our beliefs, and mathematical precision.

CHAPTER 6

More Than Metrics

Our best stat might not tell you a whole lot.
- Jason Kephart

NUMBERS ALONE DO LITTLE

In his 2007 essay on why we are obsessed with Top Ten lists, James Poniewozik offers a wonderful example of why we are drawn to numbers. His lampoon of lists is itself a list. It starts at #10 "God made us do it," which explains that our predisposition towards numbers is directly attributable to religion, i.e. The Ten Commandments, The Eightfold Path, The 95 Theses, The 613 Laws. He ends his essay, and at the same time proves his point, with #1 "Because if you put numbers on it, people will read anything, however trite, trivial and insipid, from beginning to end."[iv]

While numbers by themselves do little, integrating numbers into the ask or a case for support will inevitably make it stronger. The use of numbers in a fundraising appeal certainly fits well with the rational approach discussed in Chapter 3, although numbers standing alone are not entirely all you need to win a campaign. If they were, all we would do as a firm is crank out OVPs all day, mail them to our client's funding prospects and wait for the money to roll in. Yet it doesn't work that way and probably never will.

A thoroughly researched and well-written ROI report has never raised a dime for a nonprofit by itself, and numbers usually don't elicit an emotional response. Granted, a story will cause more of an emotional response, but that alone will not 1) appeal to the rational investor or 2) justify a solicitation for a large amount. At this point, we come full circle, in a skewed sort of way. I will agree with the conclusions of the Emotional Camp if I can add just one word: alone. The emotional studies say, "Numbers do not encourage people to give money." If we change it to, "Numbers *alone* do not encourage people to give money," then we are on the same page.

IT STARTED WITH "IMPACT"

When I started doing nonprofit ROI in the early 1990's, it was often mistakenly thought to be an analysis about the cost efficiency of a fundraising activity. Nonprofits in general thought ROI was about how much money was raised for a given effort compared to the cost of raising it. Technically this is correct, but misses the point. On a macro scale, real nonprofit ROI is about what was delivered to society for the money spent by the nonprofit. On a micro scale, it's about what an investor receives in terms of value for his or her investment. This is one reason why the term OVP was used synonymously with ROI. An OVP better described what nonprofit ROI really was.

The next iteration of the ROI movement was economic impact. This was certainly a step in the right direction, but was still limiting in its meaning. Economic impact connotes a big number with lots of zeros, and many have learned to tune it out or, even worse, view it negatively if the number isn't large enough.

While many nonprofits have integrated the word "impact" into their stump speech for funders, the fact that so many other nonprofits are doing the same thing naturally makes the word, well, less impactful. I have seen a lot of players in the nonprofit arena begin to adopt our vocabulary of investment, ROI, and value propositions. Unfortunately, it seems that the words alone are where they stop.

In every community in which I have worked there is always a local college professor that can perform the calculus necessary to determine the economic impact of a nonprofit. Some impacts are big; some are very small. But calculating the economic impact of a nonprofit using the classic tools of the trade, such as multipliers, input-output tables, local expenditures, and payroll, is not what real ROI is about. Economic impact does not begin to tell a particular nonprofit's story. Impact is not necessarily about the outcomes delivered and it certainly is not enough of a reason for people to throw money at a nonprofit. While economic impacts are included in an OVP, it is just one of many parts. Hearing some obscure number that is supposed to be representative of a nonprofit's economic impact is about as interesting to most nonprofit investors as learning the machining tolerances on their car's crankshaft. The numbers alone tell them nothing about what the organization does, or more importantly, how well they do it. Investors just want the car to move forward when they hit the gas.

When I am using the word *impact* and nonprofit in the same sentence, I mean the impact they have on people's lives, otherwise known as outcomes. I may use impact and ROI interchangeably to mean quantitative evidence of results, but these results are measured in more relatable positive outcomes that enhance lives or help to avoid societal costs, not an economic impact number that has little relevance to what a particular nonprofit delivers.

SOME MOVEMENT FORWARD: ON-LINE SOURCES

When I started teaching finance in 1987, if the average person wanted to do research on a stock or a company, he or she went to the library and dug out these thick binders filled with rather expensive subscription reports that were updated periodically. If you were lucky, the particular metric, say price/earnings ratio, on the particular company you were looking for was updated in the last bi-weekly bundle. You couldn't check these resources out of the library so you had to disassemble the giant binder and make copies if you wanted to take any sort of detail with you.

Fast-forward to the mid to late '90s and you had more information available at your fingertips than in all of those giant binders combined. From many more sources. For free. The internet changed—and continues to change—how we find and receive the details we need and want. While this may not have been a good turn of events for the old school publishers, it was a boon for the average investor in the stock market in terms of information availability. And with all that information, the American public poured billions of dollars into the financial markets and the financial firms did very well. Making information that was previously available only to those in the industry now available to everyone for free might have seemed threatening at first, but it allowed the financial markets to thrive.

The same thing happened to the world of information on nonprofits. Until the advent of the ability to search Form 990s online, pioneered by GuideStar in 1999, all funders had to go on was what the nonprofits told them. A Form 990 is an informational return in that it lists very limited amounts of useful information. Sure, it can tell you who is on the board, gross revenues, the pay of key people, etc. What it doesn't tell you is what is really important: What do they accomplish?

A step forward was when Charity Navigator started using the same Form 990 information, but put it to better use by developing ratios and implementing a rating system. Their rating system, as of this writing, evaluates nonprofits based on the areas of financial health and accountability/transparency. Their overall rating is then assigned ranging from zero (bad) to four (good) stars. The intuitive appeal is similar to the for-profit industry, where figures representing sales or debt alone do not provide the complete story. While Charity Navigator's system has not been without its critics, it did raise the bar so that other rating organizations had to move beyond the simple reporting of isolated figures.

The world of nonprofit evaluation has improved dramatically since then. It's hard not to ask, "What took so long?" That first generation of reporting information was simplistic, to say the least. The more important point is still missing: What results are these nonprofits delivering? The financial health and other broad measures of nonprofits are more helpful than no information, but even a four star rating does not ensure *Asking Rights*.

To address this seemingly glaring deficiency, new initiatives are being developed by some online rating websites. GuideStar has acquired two social impact rating organizations, Philanthropedia and Social Actions. Philanthropedia incorporated an expert review system, utilizing "over 1,400 experts" to evaluate 1,700 nonprofits in 15 different cause areas as of 2011. It utilized a proprietary research methodology "to help direct funding to groups of high-impact organizations in specific mission areas."

Social Actions was an "aggregator of peer-to-peer giving opportunities and other actionable resources from dozens of high-quality online philanthropic platforms." All of this was designed to connect "donors and volunteers with unique opportunities to make a difference."[v] GuideStar also teamed with the Better Business

74

Bureau's Wise Giving Alliance and Independent Sector on its collective Charting Impact project, which is further discussed in Chapter 8.

When a person goes to the GuideStar website, as of this writing, The Evidence of Impact section does incorporate Expert Comments, which do provide valuable insight into the organization and its operations. The number of nonprofits that have this section available, though, is limited and the experts are anonymous. An informal perusal of several Philanthropedia top nonprofits, as listed on the GuideStar site, contains no numbers at all. No reference to any numbers in a section with "Impact" in the title seems a bit baffling. In the end, they are still only offered opinions, much like a restaurant review by a food critic. The difference is that food critics make their living off their opinion and their ability to communicate that opinion, and are therefore not anonymous. From the nonprofit's perspective, these opinions are not a substitute for a value proposition and certainly could not be used with much effect in a funding solicitation.

Charity Navigator is adding a third dimension to its existing areas of financial health and accountability and transparency. In this third area, results "will count for the largest portion of the total rating score once it goes live," which will reportedly add "two significant features to this enhancement of their rating methodology."[vi]

The first improvement is the addition of collected feedback from beneficiaries, which can be, well, beneficial. The second is more troublesome in my mind: the creation of a web platform that will be used to "train, certify and guide an army of Charity Navigator raters." The stated goal is to annually evaluate the "roughly 10,000 charities that garner ~70% of the revenue that comes into the nonprofit sector each year."[vii] Charity Navigator plans on accomplishing this goal by training volunteers throughout the country, with its staff serving in a quality-control capacity.

My concern is that if this catches on and is as successful as Charity Navigator hopes it will be, the future of funding the nonprofit down the street will be influenced, and possibly even dependent, on nameless, faceless, and possibly anonymous raters.

GOING TOO FAR?

Some really push the envelope of quantitative analysis. GiveWell, for example, is considered by many to be on the extreme of quantitative analysis, but there are those who, according to GiveWell, go even further:

> "While some people feel that GiveWell puts too much emphasis on the measurable and quantifiable, there are others who go further than we do in quantification, and justify their giving (or other) decisions based on fully explicit expected-value formulas.
>
> ...We believe that people in this group are often making a fundamental mistake, one that we have long had intuitive objection to but have recently developed a more formal (though still fairly rough) critique of it. The mistake (we believe) is estimating the "expected value" of a donation (or other action) based solely on a fully explicit, quantified formula, many of whose inputs are guesses or very rough estimates. We believe that any estimate along these lines needs to be adjusted using a 'Bayesian prior'; that this adjustment can rarely be made (reasonably) using an explicit, formal calculation; and that most attempts to do the latter, even when they seem to be making a very conservative downward adjustments to the expected value of an opportunity, are not making nearly large enough downward adjustments to be consistent with the proper Bayesian approach.
>
> This view of ours illustrates why—while we seek to ground our recommendations in relevant facts, calculations and quantitative to the extent possible—every recommendation we make incorporates many different forms of evidence and involves a strong dose of intuition. And we generally prefer to give where we have strong evidence that donations can do a lot of good rather than where we have weak evidence that donations can do far more good—a preference that I believe is inconsistent with the approach of giving based on explicit expected-value formulas (at least those that (a) have

a significant room for error (b) do not incorporate Bayesian adjustments, which are very rare in these analysis and very difficult to do both formally and reasonably)."[viii]

I definitely lean towards the spectrum of demonstrating results, but even I am not as far left (or is it right?) as these folks. If I were to interject the phrase "Bayesian prior" into a conversation with a potential funder in a solicitation, no matter how sophisticated they may be, their eyes would immediately glaze over.

A better example of what GiveWell said, in plain English, is found deeper in the blog.

"Informal objections to EEV decision-making

There are many ways in which this sort of reasoning laid out above seems (to us) to fail a common sense test.

- There seems to be nothing in EEV (explicit expected-value) that penalizes relative ignorance or relatively poorly grounded estimates, or rewards investigation and the forming of particularly well-grounded estimates. I can literally save a child I see drowning by ruining a $1,000 suit, but if in the same moment I make a wild guess that this $1,000 could save two lives if given toward medical research, EEV seems to indicate that I should opt out for the latter.

- Because of this, a world in which people acted based on EEV would seem to be problematic in various ways.

- ...If you are basing your actions on EEV analysis, it seems that you're very open to being exploited by Pascal's Mugging: a tiny probability of a huge-value expected outcome can come to dominate your decision-making in ways that seem to violate common sense."[ix]

GiveWell's description offers a more academic way of saying that your value proposition should be credible, one of the three things necessary to effectively communicate your ROI. Credibility — along with objectivity and regularity — are necessary for the ROI message to gain traction with investors.

To further enhance your organization's credibility:

1. Make sure the issue passes the reasonableness test. That is, would an average person armed with the facts agree with your particular organization getting credit (maybe not all of the credit, but a significant portion of the credit)?

2. Make sure the results reported are not so fantastic that they become unbelievable. While the return per dollar invested can be very large when dealing with prevention, education, and downstream effect, it is important to use straightforward methodology that can be easily explained.[x]

PUTTING IT ALL TOGETHER

To summarize, online sources of information have come a long way, evolving from information suppliers to rating agencies. And the rating systems have gotten better, too. But, as with many discussions about the online tsunami of information, does it help the average nonprofit develop its *Asking Rights*?

Maybe. But it would require that this information be communicated to the potential funder, either directly — which puts the burden of research on the prospect — or indirectly by the fundraiser. Typically, time is at such a premium in solicitation situations that it would be difficult to inject any online information.

The practical implementation of these online sources and ratings in a fundraising context is still up for discussion. A June 2012 article in *The Chronicle of Philanthropy* entitled "Donors Say They Would Give More If They Saw More Results" describes a study of 15,000 donors (again, not test subjects with make-believe money) by Cygnus Applied Research.[xi] This is the fourth annual survey of its kind and uncovered views germane to this discussion.

*   Middle-age donors are demanding more results and want to see a clear path to where their money is going.

*   These same donors want to know that their choice of nonprofits to support is the best of all organizations working in that space.

- A "significant majority" of donors are getting more involved in the research of a particular nonprofit before they commit their money.

- Five years ago, two out of three donors engaged in research before they gave. Today, more than four out of five engage in research, and the most popular avenue is the respective nonprofit's website.

- Approximately 62 percent said they go to a charity's website for information, and almost half said they made a donation online.

- While only 36 percent went to a particular website with the intention of making a donation, 49 percent go to learn about their activities, 35 percent look to what has been accomplished with previous funding, and 23 percent look to what will be accomplished with future funding.

- Thirty-two percent of donors who were not intending to donate said they subsequently gave money because of what they learned on the website.

- Donors are far more likely to go to the charity's website than to a rating agency.[xii]

Much of this information points to the importance of a nonprofit's website and what it communicates, but the last point is especially relevant. Donors are choosing to go to a particular nonprofit's website over a third-party rating site. In the world of fundraising, this makes sense, because the potential funder already has at least a concern for the cause of a particular nonprofit, or possibly even a connection to the nonprofit itself, or they would not be visiting the website.

In the context of Kay Sprinkle Grace's Motivational Pyramid, which is found in her book *Beyond Fundraising* and shown in Exhibit 6.1, this evidence also makes sense. Many nonprofits make the mistake of starting at the wrong end of the Motivational Pyramid, the capacity end, which represents those who simply have the ability to stroke a big check. This is a fundamental, and oftentimes fatal, rookie fundraising mistake. To achieve maximum success, a nonprofit needs to start with those most connected to its organization.

Exhibit 6.1 The Motivational Pyramid

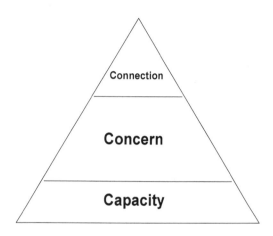

To bring all this information full circle back to the metrics debate, even though online sources are moving to outcomes/results, they are implicitly assuming that there are tens of thousands of people out there with money (capacity) searching for a deserving charity to give it to. Like the rookie mistake of a nonprofit starting at the bottom of the Motivational Pyramid, this assumption is the wrong end to use as a starting point. Ratings alone, even very high ratings, will not raise substantial amounts of money for any given nonprofit. The burden of effort lies with the nonprofit to combine Fundraising 101 with metrics that matter.

So, it is not about the search for the "golden metric" that will allow dollars to flow to the nonprofit that proves it has the most impact. It is not about third party research and rankings. It is not about the esoteric discussion of global impact. It is about how to quantify your outcomes and determine their value in a way that helps investors understand how their involvement with your organization will lead to mission fulfillment. It's all about the outcomes.

REFERENCES

[i] "GuideStar Announces Plans to Acquire Innovative Startups Philanthropedia and Social Actions," *GuideStar Press Release*, March 17, 2011.

[ii] "Where We Are Headed," *Charity Navigator*, Retrieved Aug. 8, 2011, from http://www.charitynavigator.org/index.cfm?bay=content.view&cpid=1193#.UfrOpunD-M8

[iii] "About GiveWell," *GiveWell.com*, Retrieved July 5, 2013, from http://www.givewell.org/about

[iv] James Poniewozik "The Power of 10," *Time* (December 24, 2007): 96.

[v] "Where We Are Headed," *Charity Navigator*, Retrieved Aug. 8, 2011, from http://www.charitynavigator.org/index.cfm?bay=content.view&cpid=1193#.UfrOpunD-M8

[vi] Ibid.

[vii] Ibid.

[viii] Holden, "Why We Can't Take Expected Value Estimates Literally (Even When They're Unbiased)," *The GiveWell Blog*, Retrieved on August 12, 2011.

[ix] Ibid.

[x] Tom Ralser, ROI for Nonprofits: The New Key to Sustainability (Hoboken: John Wiley & Sons, 2007).

[xi] Raymund Flandez (June 21, 2012), "Donors Say They Would Give More If They Saw More Results," *The Chronicle of Philanthropy,* Retrieved on June 21, 2012 from http://philanthropy.com/article/Many-Donors-Would-Give-More-if/132437/

[xii] Penelope Burke, The Cygnus Donor Survey: Where Philanthropy is headed in 2012 (Chicago: Cygnus Applied Research, June 2012) 41.

Terms in This Chapter

SIF (Social Innovation Fund)

Established in 2009, SIF is an initiative of the Corporation for National and Community Service under the Edward M. Kennedy Serve America Act, which "uses limited federal investment as a catalyst to grow community-based nonprofits with evidence of strong results."[i] Each dollar donated is matched by a grant maker and again by the nonprofit organization selected for the grant.

CHAPTER 7

More Than Measurement

My view is that even in a world awash in information, nonprofit leaders generally don't have the benefit of the right information. By the same token, most don't have the supporting culture or encouragement to put the right information to good use in managing their mission and operations.

- Mario Morino

EVALUATION IS NOT IMPACT, MEASUREMENT IS NOT THE POINT

Measurement and evaluation, as a concept, is one of the more quickly growing fields in the nonprofit world. The measurement and evaluation folks have even spawned their own acronym: M&E. Although it sounds like for-profit mergers and acquisitions, aka M&A, the term has the right intentions. Many of the more progressive organizations have made M&E the foundation of their strategy for getting money to where it can do the most good, including Venture Philanthropy Partners, The Edna McConnell Clark Foundation, and the Robin Hood Foundation.

All of this is well and good, but the experience of being in the fundraising trenches of many nonprofits operating on less than $1 million per year has granted me a different perspective. Many of them are resistant to anything that sounds similar to evaluation or measurement, and this resistance of using an ROI-based process as the foundation of a funding effort is sometimes rooted in their past. Organizations that have depended on funding from grants, especially federally funded grants, have an overly sensitive response to words like ROI, impact and value propositions. This stems from the funding environment in which they grew up and continue to live, because many of their programs have to be periodically, if not annually, evaluated. This evaluation is often done by an expert on the subject, such as someone with a medical background for clinics or an educational background for school systems.

In these situations, a program evaluation is really an assessment of accountability not an audit in the financial sense; it's an effort to ensure that the money is being used as dictated in the grant. These assessments too often focus on activities, or outputs, and rarely go downstream to outcomes, aka the impact on the primary customer.

These evaluations are often directly tied to funding, and maintaining the current level of funding is a completely acceptable result. The consequences of a negative assessment are far more damaging: if the program is not up to par, funding can be reduced or even cut completely. In fact, many grants stipulate that an approved evaluation must take place and denote that part of the money awarded is already earmarked for that purpose when the grant arrives. The unfortunate effect on these types of nonprofits is that they then view anything remotely resembling an evaluation or measurement as being synonymous with funding, but only in a negative or threatening sense, rather than an opportunity to garner more funding.

As with the industry's embrace of a more rational approach to fundraising, so too are things looking up for evaluations. The Corporation for National and Community Service, in its effort to make funding available for nonprofits that demonstrate measurable social impact, created the Social Innovation Fund (SIF). It provides funding for organizations that apply "with at least some preliminary causal evidence of program effectiveness."[ii]

In the submission guidelines, it lists three levels of evidence that are needed for funding.

> **Strong evidence** means evidence from studies whose designs can support causal conclusions (i.e., studies with high internal validity), and studies that in total include enough of the range of participants and settings to support scaling up to the state, regional, or national level (i.e., studies with high external validity). The following are examples of strong evidence: (1) More than one well-designed and well-

implemented experimental study or well-designed and well-implemented quasi-experimental study that supports the effectiveness of the practice, strategy, or program; or (2) one large, well-designed and well-implemented randomized controlled multisite trial that supports the effectiveness of the practice, strategy, or program.

Moderate evidence means evidence from studies whose designs can support causal conclusions (i.e., studies with high internal validity), but have limited generalizability (i.e., moderate external validity), or studies with high external validity, but moderate internal validity. The following are examples of studies that could produce moderate evidence: (1) At least one well-designed and well-implemented experimental or quasi-experimental study supporting the effectiveness of the practice, strategy, or program, with a small sample size or other conditions of implementation or analysis that limit generalizability; (2) at least one well-designed and well-implemented experimental or quasi-experimental study that does not demonstrate equivalence between the intervention and comparison groups at program entry, but that has no other major flaws related to internal validity; or (3) correlational research with strong statistical controls for selection bias and for discerning the influence of internal factors.

Preliminary evidence means evidence from studies that is based on a reasonable hypothesis supported by research findings. Thus, research that has yielded promising results for either the program or a similar program will constitute preliminary evidence and will meet CNCS's criteria. Examples of research that meet the standards include:1) outcome studies that track program participants through a service pipeline and measure participants' responses at the end of the program; and 2) pre- and post-test research that determines whether participants have improved on an outcome of interest.

Don't get me wrong, evaluation of effectiveness is vitally important, especially when using tax dollars. But these guidelines ring with the burden of evaluation, not the demonstration of value. The guidelines reflect how a grantor, the entity that has a pool of dollars to distribute, views the process. Often, this pool of dollars is not necessarily their own, and many times it represents the 5 percent required by law to distribute. There is a huge difference between the writing of a grant, putting your best reasons for funding on paper, and directly asking for money in person. In a face-to-face ask situation, the dollars do not normally come from a mandated amount that has to be given away. To the contrary, they often come from marketing budgets or business development budgets that compete with all of the other options available for spending.

The important part of a funding mechanism like SIF is that it focuses attention on a program's effectiveness with and for the primary customer. *Asking Rights*, on the other hand, is more about demonstrating value to the supporting customer, the funder, rather than the primary customer. The three levels of evidence listed previously are nothing more than a list of what it takes to get their money.

Many, many respected organizations follow the ideal of funding results, and many of them are partners with SIF.[iii] One of these, Venture Philanthropy Partners, was co-founded by Mario Morino in 2000. I first met Mr. Morino in the late '90s when he was one of the leaders of a project called the Potomac Knowledge Way, an initiative designed to position the Greater Washington (DC) region as a center of digital commerce and innovation. A large part of that effort was workforce development, and some of the discussion in the various meetings I was a part of included how to harness the knowledge of retired military and government workers and how to get computers in front of inner-city kids. The idea of pairing children with computers was that even if it was dangerous to step outside of their house, a computer allowed learning to take place inside their home in relative safety.

Mr. Morino founded the Morino Institute in 1994, and he has a demonstrated record of being a big thinker in the philanthropic arena. He has championed the act of moving beyond measurement to looking towards management tools for better outcomes, an exercise that he calls "managing to outcomes." His feelings about using measurement proactively are said best in his own words.

"Managing to outcomes should be an essential part of how nonprofits function and thus covered by revenue sources, akin to how nonprofits fund their development functions or their budgetary/cost accounting.

But for this to happen, funders have to accept the necessity of providing resources to cover operational, not just project, expenses. Instead of just pushing nonprofits for 'more information on results' funders should be willing to support what it takes for nonprofit leaders to actually produce those results. And that includes investing in outcomes management, a term I prefer over 'outcomes measurement.'

...At a minimum, funders should support efforts to help nonprofits build the capacity and culture for tracking the outcomes of those served, undertake at least a basic of this information, and identify how they can use the information to improve their programs over time. For my money, these investments have a tremendous return on investment."[iv]

CONFUSING METRICS WITH VALUE PROPOSITIONS

This book is designed to be a useful tool for nonprofits in their fundraising endeavors, based on the premise that delivering valuable outcomes will attract sustainable funding. One by-product of this focus is that investors will likely *increase* funding when they are shown a relevant ROI. Another benefit is that the discussion on nonprofit metrics will be elevated to serve more useful purposes, rather than mere philosophic exercises.

The integration of value propositions and ROI-based outcomes is intended to be a tool that can dramatically improve fundraising success. It is not intended to be a method that allows comparison of one nonprofit to another, with the end result being that the nonprofit with highest expected value gets the funding. When the discussion turns to comparisons such as this, it can quickly turn esoteric and be ultimately less useful to an individual nonprofit.

The worst case scenario is when the discussion becomes distorted and turns into a macro/global/societal issue about the value of nonprofits in general. This type of discussion about metrics may start with noble means, but ends up not being useful to the average nonprofit engaged in, say, a capital campaign. At the individual nonprofit level, what matters is *how* to use metrics to help in the pursuit of funding.

Back in 2010, there was an online discussion about nonprofit metrics on SocialEdge.org, which has now been merged into the Skoll Foundation. One of the conclusions reached from the discussion, if a conclusion can be reached in an online forum with long threads, is the exact opposite of what is useful to an individual nonprofit: how do we tie metrics to funding? The comments in the thread do a good job of distilling the debate, but also illustrate how the discussion can become misdirected. Some of those who posted are highly respected people in the nonprofit world, and at least one has written a very popular book about nonprofits. I believe they all had good intentions but, in the end, the usefulness in a funding context is limited.

Let's look at some of the comments, written by several individuals and presented in chronological order with my point of view (in *italics*) immediately following each.

Metrics That Do Harm

"I think one important element to realize is that while some charitable gifts are intended to be investments in the organization, most are like a customer buying something. The donor is paying the nonprofit to execute their program.

In the for-profit world, when you buy a cup of Starbucks, you get instant feedback on whether it was a good purchase. Since in the nonprofit world you buy things on behalf of other people, who can't personally decide if it was a good buy. That drives donors to seek indications of whether their purchase was a good one. Nonprofits respond by telling stories about their beneficiaries (which works to satisfy their donors), but more and more donors want proof. This is what has led to the rise of metrics.

But in the end I think that most metrics offer a false precision."[v]

The description of the transaction is right on target. There are two value propositions in play. The evolution of the importance of metrics is also correct. The concluding statement of a false precision may also be true, depending on how one defines false precision. The subtle point is that precision is not what metrics are necessarily intended to offer, and certainly not what value propositions are intended to accomplish. Much like the stories mentioned, where the better the story the better the result, the better the value proposition the better the result. Sure, the more accuracy the better, but the process of directing funding to an organization is rarely a matter of precision, and most development directors understand this. Of the many steps in the process of successfully raising money, if the conversation becomes one of the precision of the metrics involved, the discussion has gone off of the tracks.

The above post was immediately followed by a discussion about non-isolated metrics. That is, a set of numbers that can be compared across like organizations.

Non-Isolated Metrics Can Be Useful

"…I have to be able to understand what's going under the hood. I'm also inclined to support organizations that provide more information.

…Most importantly, metrics are useful, but not useful in isolation. Analyzing the metrics of one nonprofit isn't going to get you anywhere. But analyzing comparable metrics across multiple nonprofits in a similar sector will start to see trends."[vi]

This is where the assumption that comparison of nonprofits, their efficacy and the grand quest to find the magic, universal set of metrics for easy comparison overshadows the discussion. There is no "golden metric" that can compare one nonprofit to another because each nonprofit has a different mission. Even those in the same sector likely have different primary customers, and certainly will have different geographic considerations. In the nonprofit economic development sector, for example, I have used a cost-per-job created metric for years and have developed quite a database of results. It's useful for some budgeting estimates, but the reality is that those areas where the local economy is severely depressed will have to spend more money to entice industries thus driving up their cost-per-job metrics. So a high cost-per-job metric may lead to the wrong conclusion entirely: that the nonprofit is not cost effective in creating jobs. The real insight is that although the metric might ostensibly indicate the organization is inefficient by this measure, given that the geographic area in which they are trying to improve things is starting from a much more disadvantaged and unappealing place, costs will naturally be higher.

The conversation then continued along these lines.

Measuring Impact Across a Cause

"I agree . . . 'Most importantly, metrics are useful, but not in isolation. Analyzing the metrics of one nonprofit isn't going to get you anywhere.' Unfortunately, there are few metrics that can be measured across nonprofits in the same cause, that I believe give an indication of the great work or impact a nonprofit is having. One can compare quantifiable metrics like fundraising efficiencies and overhead ratios, and perhaps things like volunteer repeat participation, but what metrics can measure impact? It is easy to measure the number of vaccines given or the number of houses built, but what about the metrics that cannot be measured easily. How do we quantify the amount a nonprofit has changed the life of an individual? How do we measure the effect a theatre performance has had on a 6th grader? These are equally important measures, I believe.

I believe there is even more power in understanding the relative impact of a nonprofit to others in the field. However, as just one person without a ton of knowledge in a particular cause I care about, say the performing arts, how can I possibly make those comparisons myself? How much data, due diligence, and time would I have to gather and spend in order to feel good about my $100 or $1,000 donation? And is it realistic that I would spend any time at all?[vii]

I could not have paid this person to respond better: "…what metrics measure impact," "these are equally important measures" and "is it realistic that I would really spend any time at all?" The response focused correctly on outputs verses outcomes and their associated value, it just used different words. This is exactly why the burden of impact is squarely on the shoulders of the nonprofit, and what better vehicle to evaluate if that impact is credible and is being communicated correctly than a fundraising campaign?

The next post then shifts the entire argument.

To Move Beyond Metrics, Change Your Unit of Analysis

"The problem is, the discussion is framed around an impossible goal. Even if the donors and the nonprofits they fund figure out the "right" metrics and more resources flow to a relative handful of nonprofits achieving the greatest impact, we will be missing the boat. We will still be looking for ways to differentiate between "good" and "bad" nonprofits – picking winners and losers.

…I'd like to see the conversation shift from rating individual nonprofits and focus instead on how more donors and nonprofits can together begin to measure their collective contributions across a field, cause, or 'ecosystem.'

The difference here is that donors are using their funding to produce alignment and synergy among nonprofits, rather than fanning the flames of competition between cash-strapped nonprofits that already spend too much time vying for scarce grant dollars. By taking a field-wide view, they've shifted the unit of analysis away from single nonprofits to defining and advancing outcomes across the entire field."[viii]

Competition among nonprofits is not, by definition, a bad thing. It seems to work in the for-profit sector pretty well. And most nonprofits with Asking Rights do not rely solely on grants. But beyond that, the argument that certain nonprofits are higher performing is true.

After reading just four posts on the topic of metrics, in just one thread in one forum, it's easy to see how the pros and cons of metrics gets a bit academic.

ROI IS NOT THE SAME AS MEASUREMENT

Demonstrating ROI is not a magic bullet for funding, just as metrics are not a magic bullet for better management. They can be very important parts of the solution, but they are not a solution unto themselves.

In the early '90s, using the term "ROI" was even less popular than using the terms "investor" or "investment." Fortunately, these terms are now more accepted, but the true meaning of these words seems to have been lost. ROI, like the words "impact" or "effectiveness," are often reduced to the thinness of tissue paper by overuse, misuse, and abuse. These words are typically used as advertisement tag lines or sound bites, not as real models of how programs deliver value. Unfortunately, nonprofit ROI is still defined by many to be a comparison of the cost spent on the most recent golf tournament or black tie gala compared to how much money was raised. This works for the internal accountants, but not for those you expect to fund your nonprofit. They are interested in the impact you have on society and on the outcomes you deliver.

Mathematically, ROI is return divided by investment. The investment part is easy, the return part can be more subjective than many would like.

The bottom line is, too much emphasis on metrics, measurement, impact, or assessment can have unintended consequences. Former Ford Foundation President Susan Berresford has said that the insistence for grantees to demonstrate measurable, short-term impact can have a "miniaturizing ambition" effect, causing an aversion to break-through work because it is too risky or may take too long for results to surface.[ix] Dr. Sanjoy Mahajan states in his book *Street-Fighting Mathematics: The Art of Educated Guessing and Opportunistic Problem Solving*, that "too much rigor teaches rigor mortis: the fear of making an unjustified leap even when it lands on a correct result."[x] This is how a mathematician says the same thing that Mr. Marino is saying: too much emphasis on the measurement and not using that information to achieve better results misses the point entirely.

REFERENCES

[i] "Social Innovation Fund," Corporation for National & Community Service Website, Retrieved on September 3, 2012, from www.nationalservice.gov/about/programs/innovation.asp

[ii] "Social Innovation Fund: Content Requirements for Subgrantee Evaluation Plans," Corporation for National & Community Services, February 2012, 6.

[iii] Ashley Allen (September 28, 2011). "Innovations in Measurement and Evaluation," *Philanthropy News Digest*, Retrieved September 28, 2011, from http://foundationcenter.org/pnd/impact/impact_item.jhtml?id=355100010

[iv] Mitch Nauffts (January 28, 2012). "5 Questions for... Mario Morino, Co-Founder/Chair, Venture Philanthropy Partners," *Philanthropy News Digest*, Retrieved August 28, 2012, from http://foundationcenter.org/pnd/fivequestions/5q_item.jhtml?id=368300003

[v] Sean Stannard-Stockton, "Metrics That Do Harm," Post in Discussions Thread: "Nonprofit Analysis, Beyond Metrics," by Sean Stannard-Stockton, *SocialEdge.org*, September 29, 2010, Retrieved from http://skollworldforum.org/2010/09/08/nonprofit-analysis-beyond-metrics/

[vi] David Lynn, "Non-Isolated Metrics Can Be Useful," Post in Discussions Thread: "Nonprofit Analysis, Beyond Metrics," by Sean Stannard-Stockton, *SocialEdge.org*, September 29, 2010, Retrieved from http://skollworldforum.org/2010/09/08/nonprofit-analysis-beyond-metrics/

[vii] Erin Andrews, "Measuring Impact Across a Cause," Post in Discussions Thread: "Nonprofit Analysis, Beyond Metrics," by Sean Stannard-Stockton, *SocialEdge.org*, September 29, 2010, Retrieved from http://skollworldforum.org/2010/09/08/nonprofit-analysis-beyond-metrics/

[viii] Leslie Crutchfield, "To Move Beyond Metrics, Change Your Unit of Analysis," Post in Discussions Thread: "Nonprofit Analysis, Beyond Metrics," by Sean Stannard-Stockton, *SocialEdge.org*, September 29, 2010, Retrieved from http://skollworldforum.org/2010/09/08/nonprofit-analysis-beyond-metrics/

[ix] Steven Lawry (July 12, 2010). "When Too Much Rigor Leads to Rigor Mortis: Valuing Experience, Judgment, and Intuition in Nonprofit Management," *Hausercenter.org*, Retrieved September 5, 2011, from http://hausercenter.org/iha/2010/07/12/when-too-much-rigor-leads-to-rigor-mortis-valuing-experience-judgment-and-intuition-in-nonprofit-management/

[x] Dr. Sanjoy Mahajan, *Street-Fighting Mathematics: The Art of Educated Guessing and Opportunistic Problem Solving*, (Cambridge: MIT Press, 2010), 99.

Section 2 Introduction
Developing Your Asking Rights

The first section introduced the concept, framed the discussion and built the case for <u>why</u> *Asking Rights* are important. This second section focuses on <u>how</u> to develop your *Asking Rights*, and introduces the ingredients and process of a successful funding program to fit today's nonprofit investors.

You can look at the *Asking Rights* formula as the basic ingredients, and the Investment-Driven Model™ (hereinafter referred to as "Investment-Driven Model" without the trademark symbol used to facilitate readability) as the recipe for combining those ingredients into an effective funding effort. The outcomes you deliver are a part of both, and Investable Outcomes™ (hereinafter referred to as "Investable Outcomes" without the trademark symbol used to facilitate readability) are introduced as the unique way to make your program of work appealing to investors. All of the chapters in this section are designed to help build the basics of an investment-driven program based on the outcomes you deliver.

Part 1 The Ingredients
C+F+O

Ch. 8 Something Old is New Again
These important questions are a good place to start

Ch. 9 The *Asking Rights* Formula
The ingredients necessary to establish Asking Rights

Part 2 The Process
Discovering, Translating, Matching, Using

Ch. 10 The Investment-Driven Model and Investable Outcomes
Outcomes are why investors (people) invest (give)

Ch. 11 Driving the IDM Further
More on why the IDM is successful

Ch. 12 Do You Have *Asking Rights*?
What organizations told us about themselves

Terms in This Chapter

Peter Drucker (1909-2005)
A writer, professor, and management consultant, described by *BusinessWeek* as "the man who invented management."[i]

Better Business Bureau (BBB)
BBB's mission is to be the leader in advancing marketplace trust.[ii]

Wise Giving Alliance
A program of the BBB, the Wise Giving Alliance helps donors make informed giving decisions and promotes high standards of conduct among organizations that solicit contributions from the public.[iii]

Independent Sector
A nonprofit that seeks to advance the common good by leading, strengthening, and mobilizing the nonprofit and philanthropic community.[iv]

CHAPTER 8

Something Old is New Again

When a subject becomes totally obsolete we make it a
required course.

- Peter Drucker

THE MASTER IS STILL RELEVENT

Although Peter Drucker is most widely known for his philosophical
and practical thoughts on the modern for-profit corporation,
authoring 39 books on the subject in total, he also made some
enduring contributions to the nonprofit world. *The Five Most
Important Questions You Will Ever Ask About Your Nonprofit
Organization*, more recently re-published as *The Drucker Foundation
Self-Assessment Tool*, is a valuable exercise that every nonprofit
organization should take advantage of in their annual board
retreat.[v]

Drucker's five questions are:

1. What Is Our Mission?
2. Who Is Our Customer?
3. What Does Our Customer Value?
4. What Are Our Results?
5. What Is Our Plan?

Drucker's questions are easy to understand, direct, and to the point.
Questions #3 and #4 in particular are extremely valuable to the
discussion of *Asking Rights*. Understanding what the customer
values and using this information to deliver results that matter to
them are the essence of *Asking Rights*, so let's look at these questions
more closely.

Question #3 - What Does Our Customer Value?

Drucker divides customers into two groups: primary customers whose lives are changed through the organization's efforts, and supporting customers who make the mission possible, such as staff, volunteers, board member, and investors. I only know of one way to determine what either customer values...

ASK THEM!

This, of course, is the premise of a feasibility study. Even though the executive director may be brilliant, the board may be overflowing with wisdom, and the development people may be the best in the business, none of them are omniscient. This vital information — what the customer values — simply cannot be determined in a vacuum.

Now, discovering what the primary customer values may surprise you. Drucker himself tells the story of how a homeless shelter assumed their primary customers valued nutritious meals and clean beds. After face-to-face interviews with them, the shelter came to understand that, while food and beds were appreciated, "they do little or nothing to satisfy the deep aspiration not to be homeless."[vi] Simply put, the primary customer did not want to feel homeless. The organization then devised new strategies to deliver what the primary customer valued, including the ability to stay at the shelter for longer periods of time and a safer environment. This, of course, requires more of a commitment from the primary customer, but the organization's results are also improved.

Whereas determining what the primary customer values may help improve operations, shape strategy, and fulfill missions, determining what the supporting customer values may be the difference between keeping the doors open or closing up shop. If funders do not feel what they value is important to the organization, funding may stop. As mentioned, this is why a feasibility study is done as a first step before a campaign is launched, and why there is a promise of confidentiality in the feasibility process so that there is no reason to fear reprisal for any comments made.

Question #4 - What Are Our Results?

Results, whether qualitative or quantitative, are becoming more important by the minute in our 24/7 world of instant information. In the nonprofit world, results are measured outside of the organization, by the impact on the primary customer, and are being reported to a completely different faction, the supporting customers.

Every organization, for-profit or nonprofit, has internal measures, standards, and goals. Internal measures are often so specific to the industry that an outsider might not even understand the words. Spend enough time around production facilities, health care providers, the military, or a technology campus and you will instantly know what I mean. For nonprofits, it is important that the communication of these results is in a language that the investor understands, not in the language of the organization.

Every for-profit also has external measures that need to be reported, sometimes to shareholders or owners, and always to the government. The top line is as important as the bottom line: revenue, profitability and, in the case of public corporations, earnings per share. These measures are what drive the outside world's view of the health of the company and, ultimately, its value. If earnings are down, it's a safe bet that the stock price will be also.

In the case of nonprofits, the consequences of reporting external results is not that different. This is never more obvious than when asking someone for money. Everyone has an opinion, but the most important opinions are those that are offered by potential funders. With that in mind, it is critical to include people in a feasibility study who aren't yet connected or close to the organization and who have not yet made an investment. So many organizations make the mistake of only talking to those who are fans and current funders, but this tactic misses a tremendous opportunity to create awareness among new, potential investors and to gain insight on what this new group values. Outside opinion, especially on the outcomes delivered by the organization, is just as important to nonprofits as for-profits. They drive the community's view of the organization's health. And they drive investment too.

Let's summarize the relevance of the above two questions:

1. *Asking Rights* deal with the supporting customers, most notably the funders of an organization.

2. The results that matter for the purpose of developing *Asking Rights* are those that matter to the investors.

And while these two questions are a great place to start the process of developing your *Asking Rights*, there are also other lists of questions that have entered the arena of nonprofit impact… and it's about time. The Independent Sector, BBB's Wise Giving Alliance, and GuideStar USA have jointly developed a set of inquiries as part of a Charting Impact project/product.[vii] From the website:

> "Donors care that your organization is making a difference, but often have a hard time finding information about the impact your organization has been having. Charting Impact helps your organization tell your story in an accessible, concise way by answering **five simple yet powerful questions.**
>
> Charting Impact encourages strategic thinking about how you will achieve your goals. It also creates a report that lets you share concise, detailed information about plans and progress with key stakeholders, including the public. It was designed with several benefits in mind, including:
>
> - Encouraging people to invest their money, time, and attention in effective organizations;
> - Helping your organization highlight the difference you make;
> - Positioning your organization to work with and learn from other organizations; and
> - Helping your organization sharpen your approaches to making a difference."

The five questions of Charting Impact are:

1. What is your organization aiming to accomplish?

2. What are your strategies for making this happen?

3. What are your organization's capabilities for doing this?

4. How will your organization know if you are making progress?

5. What have and haven't you accomplished so far?

When Drucker's questions are placed next to Charting Impact's, in a slightly different order as shown in Exhibit 8.1, the similarities become clear.

Exhibit 8.1 Question Comparison

Charting Impact	Drucker
#1 – What is your organization aiming to accomplish?	#1 – What is Our Mission?
#2 – What are your strategies for making this happen?	#5 – What is Our Plan?
#3 – What are your organization's capabilities for doing this?	#1 – What is Our Mission? (*What Are Our Opportunities?*) and #4 – What Are Our Results? (*What Should We Strengthen or Abandon?*)
#4 – How will your organization know if you are making progress?	#4 – What Are Our Results? (*How Should We Define Results?*)
#5 – What have and haven't you accomplished so far?	#4 – What Are Our Results? (*Are We Successful?*)

The importance of this exercise is what you do with the answers to the questions, no matter how they are phrased, in order to make your organization more financially sustainable.

GOOD SEATS STILL AVAILABLE ON THE BANDWAGON

Regardless of who is extolling the virtues of an ROI-based approach, the good news is that these types of approaches are gaining ground. The bad news is that much of the advice being doled out is coming from a rather academic perspective, i.e. the way things should be, not the way things really are. One of the more recent entrants into the ROI = funding arena is the book *The End of Fundraising*. While the author, Jason Saul, was kind enough to mention *ROI for Nonprofits* in his preface, he erroneously lumps it in with a list of books that he claims "are written for a different paradigm — a world in which nonprofits live outside of the economy."

Immediately following this list of books that he says miss the point, he offers seven suggestions that support his argument. The last five are:

- Define your impact by outcomes, not activities.
- Determine which stakeholders value your outcomes the most.
- Translate your work into high-value outcomes.
- Create powerful value propositions to increase your leverage.
- Improve the success of your pitch to funders.

Just for grins, compare those bullets with the Five Steps to Demonstrating Value (shown below) from the first section of the chapter entitled Building an OVP for your Organization in *ROI for Nonprofits,* which was first published in 2004 as 5 Steps to Building an Organizational Value Proposition.

1. Determine the motivations of your stakeholders.
2. Develop a program with definable outcomes.
3. Translate outcomes into specific benefits.
4. Demonstrate effectiveness in investment terms.
5. Report results on a regular basis.

My list followed a chapter on the need to move beyond output (activities) to outcomes (impact), and from outcomes to their value to get the most traction with funders. It is nice to see that someone else in the nonprofit space agrees with these fundraising concepts, even if they are not in the business of actually raising money for their clients.

Making Sense of All of This

No matter which set of questions you choose to use, they will help you understand more about your organization and provide a good launching pad for what lies ahead. And while some might find them more useful for strategy development or mission evaluation, the questions are also invaluable in developing *Asking Rights*, since these rights are earned by combining credibility, outcomes and fundraising skills.

Key points to remember are:

- Knowing what your supporting customers value will influence your credibility;

- The results, or outcomes, you choose to highlight will influence the amount of the ask; and

- Translating your outcomes into benefits that matter to your investors is an important part — perhaps the most important part — of the fundraising process.

REFERENCES

[i] "Peter Drucker's Life and Legacy," *The Drucker Institute*, Retrieved July 2013, from http://www.druckerinstitute.com/link/about-peter-drucker/
[ii] "Vision, Mission and Values," *Better Business Bureau*, Retrieved July 2013, from http://www.bbb.org/us/mission-and-values/
[iii] "About BBB Wise Giving Alliance," *Better Business Bureau*, Retrieved July 2013, from http://www.bbb.org/us/Wise-Giving/
[iv] "IS Vision, Mission, and Values," *Independent Sector,* Retrieved July 2013, from http://www.independentsector.org/mission_and_values
[v] The Peter F. Drucker Foundation for Nonprofit Management, *The Drucker Foundation Self-Assessment Tool*, (New York: Jossey-Bass, Inc., 1999), 5.
[vi] Ibid. 33.
[vii] "Charting Impact," *Independent Sector.* Retrieved on October 2012, from http://www.independentsector.org/charting_impact

CHAPTER 9

The *Asking Rights* Formula

If you can't explain it simply, you don't understand it
well enough.
- Albert Einstein

THE GENESIS

Over the course of 18 years and 500+ projects in this business, I've
seen certain patterns emerge. Sometimes funding projects succeed
wildly, sometimes they are more difficult than anticipated, and
sometimes they are long, arduous tasks that slog along and need to
be put out of their misery. Every campaign is indeed different, as is
every organization, every board, and every circumstance.

On an individual project basis, it is relatively easy to see why things
succeed. In fact, the pattern becomes quite clear.

- The steps in the process were followed.
- The steps were executed well.
- No steps were skipped.
- Motivations to invest were uncovered.
- The program of work was focused on outcomes.
- The board was strong.
- The right leadership was recruited.
- The correct evaluations of likely financial participation were
  used.
- The ask was made with the right ingredients in place.

On the post-mortem flip side, when each effort is examined
individually, it is also relatively easy to see what went wrong. The
obvious answers are that steps were skipped or not executed well,

the program of work was weak, the board was not supportive, and the right leadership was not enlisted. It's not uncommon that a funding effort is designed to fail, where a board pre-ordains that there will be a $10 million campaign even though the feasibility study discovers that only $4 million is possible. In other instances, the issue may have been an executive who was considered a loose cannon, a campaign may be called off due to poor organizational timing, or the economy might not be in alignment.

On a collective basis, it is more difficult to distill all of these variations of possibilities as to why some situations succeed while others fail. But, out of professional curiosity and as an internal management tool, I started to catalog the issues. I thought, perhaps, I was missing something so obvious because it was so enormous that it blocked my view of the bigger picture.

As I went through all of the projects over the years, in good economies and bad, in urban and rural areas and across all types of organizations from arts and culture to health to economic development, I asked, "Why did this project succeed effortlessly while this other one squeaked by?" And, on the rare occasion, I asked "Why did this one fail?"

The genesis of what follows is rooted in results and based on experience, not theory. So, as summarized as I can make it without losing anything important along the way, it comes down to this:

Outcomes + Credibility = *Asking Rights*

As a fundraiser, if I am armed with meaningful Outcomes and the organization has Credibility, I am almost sure to reach the goal. Because of what Outcomes really are and what Credibility really represents, I have earned the right to ask someone for money. For those of you who read the Introduction, with these two factors in my hip pocket, the Colonel Sanders banker would never have had to question me before he made an investment.

Yet to turn *Asking Rights* into sustainable funding, to fully realize them, it also takes the addition of Fundraising Skills. To be sure, Fundraising Skills alone do not give an organization *Asking Rights*. In fact, there are many organizations that have great fundraising skill sets and have very much mastered the art of raising money, but are sorely lacking in the Outcomes or Credibility categories. It will catch up to them. But, in order to monetize *Asking Rights*, Fundraising Skills are necessary. This is in sharp contrast to some of the other "impact experts" who feel that as long as the numbers are impactful enough, the money will roll in. So now we must add to the equation:

Asking Rights + Fundraising Skills = Sustainable Funding

Substituting Outcomes and Credibility, we get:

Outcomes + Credibility + Fundraising Skills = Sustainable Funding

Too much? Too simplified? At the risk of being accused of incorrect arithmetic, I will take some theoretical license and restate it this way:

Credibility + Fundraising Skills + Outcomes = *Asking Rights*

Or

$$C + F + O = AR$$

CFO seems much easier to remember, given its metaphorical similarity to those that manage money. Without too much license, it encompasses the meaning and focus of *Asking Rights*: being able to monetize outcomes for sustainable funding. Each variable can be thought of as a leg on a three-legged stool: if one is missing, the stool will fall over.

While deceptively simple, it has proven to be true over time and for hundreds of organizations. If all three legs are present, the fundraising effort has a much greater probability of being successful.

C = *Credibility* of the Organization

Definition:	*The quality or power of inspiring belief*
Critical Fundraising Advantage:	*It gets you in the door*
Time Reference:	*Past and/or present*
Encompasses:	*Visibility in the community, previous fundraising efforts, board strength, executive leadership, strength of brand*

It has often been said that the credibility of an organization is what gets a fundraiser in the door. This point is difficult to argue and, as a generalized statement, it is true. A foot in the door, when combined with the other two variables of the *Asking Rights* equation, more often than not allows for substantial dollars to be raised. To further the definition, credibility is an almost unshakeable belief that the organization does good things.

For an example based on personal experience, I am drawn to Goodwill Industries because of their credibility. They have convinced me over the years that they do good things with my donations of clothing, sporting equipment, household items, etc. They make it easy for me to drop things off, even to the point of providing a covered drive-through. They hand me a receipt that allows me to go online and have a permanent history of my donations. I literally can pull up, unload, and be off in a minute or less.

On their website, they have a Donation Impact Calculator that gives me instant feedback on my actions. That feedback contains the name of a real person, a picture of that person (so they are hitting on the emotional cylinders), and a statistic that tells me what my donation will do, such as 50 minutes of financial planning classes for Ms. Johnson or 2.5 hours of a job search class for Mr. Smith.

This nice touch may make me feel better about my decision to donate to them versus some other organization, but it is not what brings me to the website. I went there because of previous credibility that was established long ago and is reinforced constantly. I am sure others have shared the same experience: Goodwill's credibility is well established.

A nonprofit branding consultant once told me that a nonprofit's brand is embodied in the feeling I get when I hear the organization's name. In the case of Goodwill, I indeed feel that they do good things. They reinforce their credibility with outcomes, thus ensuring that I will continue to give them my support.

F = *Fundraising* Skills

Definition ("skills"):	*The ability to use one's knowledge effectively and readily in execution or performance*[ii]
Critical Fundraising Advantage:	*It closes the deal*
Time Reference:	*Present*
Encompasses:	*Campaign structure, process management, cultivation, leadership recruitment, correct evaluations, ability to leverage investments, the ask*

This second critical component is what allows the other two components — Credibility and Outcomes — to be monetized.

The types of Fundraising Skills I am referring to are:

Overall Campaign Management
This is the skill of herding all of the cats involved in a campaign. Campaigns, even when managed by outside professionals, still belong to the organization. It is their campaign, not that of the outside counsel or consultants. The 'cats' are those leaders who are the names and faces of the effort, most of whom have day jobs and limited time to devote to the nonprofit. Remember, these leaders are volunteers who represent supporting customers and, more importantly, they are your investors.

Leadership Cultivation

Leadership is so important to the success of the campaign, but even the best leaders will not earn the organization *Asking Rights* if the other components are missing. Much of the early stages in a campaign are spent getting the right people involved because, without them, campaigns can be very difficult.

Leadership Enlistment

This is "signing them up" in two distinct respects: their commitment to the effort and their financial commitment. In most cases, they cannot be leaders of the campaign unless they are also investors.

Correct Evaluation of Prospects

This is the skill that ensures no money is left on the table. After all, it is easy to get $1,000 from someone who really has $500,000 potential. Since everyone calibrates to the leaders, it is vitally important that the leaders are asked for the correct amounts or the campaign could be doomed from the start.

Interpersonal Skills

These are the skills of communication, the ease with which someone presents themselves, the ability to listen, the art of conversation, the ability to build rapport, etc. These skills are always important when asking someone for something, and are especially important when asking someone for money. Self-confidence and pride in one's appearance, though basic, also fall into this category.

Ability to Leverage Investments

One investment from one prospect can be used as leverage for others, beyond the basic "matching grant" or "challenge pledge." For example, if one financial institution is interested, others will also be interested.

Organizational Skills

Although it may sound easy, the task of scheduling appointments and juggling meetings can be daunting. In a typical campaign, there may be anywhere from 80 to 140 investors, which means probably 200 different prospects. If each one is met with three times, that's 600 meetings over the course of several months. Add to that the fact that each meeting takes prep work, travel time, etc., and you can see how important this skill set is.

Ability to Make the Ask

Hint: Many people are not good at this. In order to raise money, you have to ask for it. Simple to say, difficult to do. In fact, while it is often said the number one fear is speaking in front of a group, my bet is that asking someone for money is right up there.

O = *Outcomes*

Definition:	*Something that follows as a result or consequence*[iii]
Critical Fundraising Advantage:	*It justifies the amount of the investment*
Time Reference:	*Past, present, and/or future*
Encompasses:	*Ability to deliver, effectiveness of operations, implementation, focus, strategy, communication of results*

As a review, outputs are typically measures of activity, whereas outcomes are the impact an organization has on its primary customer. These are my working definitions, but to be more thorough, we can reference those in *The Nonprofit Outcomes Toolbox*.

Output – What your program or organization produces; it is your product.

Outcome – The direct, intended beneficial effect on the stakeholders or interests the organization and its programs exist to serve.

If the program is what we *do* and the output is the *product* of what we do, the outcome is what happens *because* of that product.[iv]

In fundraising, outcomes are what raise the ante in the fundraising game, and justify the amount of the ask. They are a critical component of *Asking Rights*, and if they are based on past accomplishments, they must add to the credibility of the organization. However, to be most effective in a fundraising context, they need to represent what new investment will facilitate.

From a fundraising context, the following are *not* outcomes:

- Building a new facility;
- Recruiting and training staff volunteers;
- Purchasing or upgrading equipment;
- Number of participants served;
- Participant satisfaction;
- Number of classes held;
- Workshop attendance;
- Acres conserved;
- Number of children who passed through the facility; or
- Brochures distributed.

From that same fundraising context, the following *are* outcomes:

- Children born healthy because of proper prenatal care;
- Jobs created because of industrial recruiting efforts;
- Youth who developed an appreciation of the arts and became professional artists because of early exposure and access to museums and galleries;
- Kids not arrested because of proactive afterschool programs;
- Population increases in ducks because of the numbers of acres of wetlands conserved;
- Increases in earnings of graduates because what they learned in the program made them more employable;

- People living longer lives because of the education that helped them make healthier choices; and

- Workers able to retain their job—or get promoted—because of the training delivered.

REAL WORLD EXAMPLES

To illustrate the practicality of the C+F+O formula, I offer three examples of success and three examples of struggle.

Examples of Success

Nonprofit #1

Type of Organization:	*Value-added Transitional Housing*
Campaign Goal:	*$6.5 million*
Strongest Component:	*Credibility*

This organization had been operating on a small scale for years and the demand for its services had long outpaced its ability to supply them. They had a program with a track record of success, and had cultivated friends throughout the region. When the executive director, who had been there from the beginning, decided it was time to make the leap to a much larger facility, credibility is what allowed that effort to successfully launch and turn into reality.

Because the organization, although small, had a wide-spread reputation for successful programs, the precious time spent with a potential investor was not wasted on background or history. It allowed real conversations to be initiated. In this case, the credibility of the organization was the ingredient that allowed appointments to be scheduled, conversations to be productive, motivations to be uncovered, and successful asks to be made.

Nonprofit #2

Type of Organization:	*National Sports Hall of Fame*
Campaign Goal:	*$6 million*
Strongest Component:	*Fundraising Skills*

The facility itself was old, the roof leaked, and the air conditioning needed repair. Exhibits needed to be brought into the 21st century. The executive director was very serious about his job, to the point of studying, reading, and even getting a degree in fundraising. To the detriment of the campaign, there were internal politics that hampered the effort for facility upgrades, which is not unusual since the leadership was spread throughout the country while the facility itself was in one place and traveling there was not easy.

What allowed this project to be successful was the fundraising skills of the executive director. The outcomes, in this case, could be considered the weakest of the three variables. Sure, he needed some outside help, but his natural instincts were right on target and his early cultivation of potential prospects are what allowed the project to eventually be funded.

Nonprofit #3

Type of Organization:	*Youth Services*
Campaign Goal:	*$1.35 million*
Strongest Component:	*Outcomes*

When this organization decided that it would like to have its own facilities, rather than waste money renting time at facilities owned by others, potential investors balked. They referenced the mission of the organization, saying that it might appear "exclusive" if the organization was to waste time and money on its own facility instead of focusing all resources on the outreach program. (These were facts that were uncovered in the feasibility study and allowed the campaign message to be crafted so it was successful.)

While a much smaller amount of money than originally envisioned was successfully raised, the Outcomes were subsequently delivered, and the Credibility earned in the process allowed even more money to be raised in Phase II of the campaign. The second phase was simply a scaled down version of the original project, ultimately getting the organization to where it intended. This success was made possible by delivering Outcomes that were valuable to investors.

Examples of Struggle

Nonprofit #1

Type of Organization:	*Museum of Art and Science*
Campaign Goal:	*$6.5 million*
Weakest Component:	*Credibility*

They had a great physical location, were housed in a capital city, and seemed to have their act together. But internal politics dragged this campaign down. The arts constituency and the science constituency didn't quite see eye to eye. Because the project had to appease both sides, mediocrity ensued and resources were spread too thin to thrive in either area, damaging credibility. Prospective investors interpreted this as a problem never being solvable and therefore withheld their dollars.

Nonprofit #2

Type of Organization:	*International Institution of Higher Education*
Campaign Goal:	*$2 million*
Weakest Component:	*Fundraising Skills*

This large, international school had quick growth, a great reputation for a quality product, and ever expanding enrollment. In the *Asking Rights* formula, they certainly had the Credibility and the Outcomes. Why were the results of the Development Department considered lackluster?

The answer: the Development Department. For one, there was constant turnover in staff. In a situation where investors had to be groomed over long periods of time, which is not unusual for an institution of higher education, the turnover in staff meant funders had to re-introduce themselves and reconnect with the institution time and time again. They also tended to confuse marketing with fundraising. Sure their fundraising pieces were beautiful, with gorgeous pictures and flowing prose. But fundraising relies on a much more personal relationship than that. Smart—fiscally capable—investors see past the shiny, glossy marketing glitz. With Fundraising Skills missing from the formula, *Asking Rights* couldn't be fully monetized, no matter how good the Outcomes or Credibility.

Nonprofit #3

Type of Organization:	*Startup Health Services*
Campaign Goal:	*$6.5 million*
Weakest Component:	*Outcomes*

This organization had big dreams. Too big. They wanted to make their community "the healthiest in the world." They had no track record to back this up, no experience to speak of, and appeared to lack the resources to implement their vision. Most importantly, they needed specific Outcomes that people valued.

While good health is a universal attribute that everyone can get behind, asking someone to fund such a "long shot" seemed like a bad bet. They needed small victories on which to build before they went for the big dollars, and they needed to deliver Outcomes along the way.

This organization, located in a medium-sized city, had its financial struggles before, and the recession that began in 2008 did not help matters. The funding effort never achieved lift-off.

THE HYPOTHETICAL NONPROFIT

The above examples are real. Let me present a hypothetical situation, one that is not uncommon and comes up short on two of the three variables. Let's say an organization has a strong religious affiliation and ministers to the poor in underdeveloped countries. Its efforts are, in effect, missionary, but it operates as an aid organization. The organization has the purest of intentions.

Their religious affiliation lends them immediate Credibility. Without meaning to sound sacrilegious, God is on their side and their congregation keeps them funded... but at very low levels.

Why are they underfunded, at least in their eyes?

1. They are woefully short on Outcomes, or rather the communication of their Outcomes. They feel that since their primary goal is to spread the word of God, the Outcomes that appeal to the rational investor are just not that important.

2. Their Fundraising Skills are nonexistent. They often have two collections per service. The first is for specific mission aid and the second is for ongoing operations. Almost without fail, the second collection is smaller and yet, without money to support the operation, the mission for which money was collected in the first go-round cannot be accomplished. To put it simply: two emotional appeals, especially back to back, does not a full coffer make.

This organization might be much better off if it took a more deliberate approach, documenting the organization's Outcomes and applying some interpersonal skills in its fundraising process. Rather than rely exclusively on the spiritual theme, there are certainly those in the congregation who would give more if some Outcomes were presented.

Paying attention to the C, the F and the O—and combining them to earn the organization the right to ask investors for money—is the most effective way I have found to bring sustainable dollars into a nonprofit. But these are simply the ingredients, not the recipe. In the next section, we start combining them for success.

REFERENCES

[i] "Credibility," *Merriam-Webster Dictionary*, Retrieved on March 17, 2013 from http://www.merriam-webster.com/dictionary/credibility
[ii] "Skill," *Merriam-Webster Dictionary*, Retrieved on March 17, 2013 from http://www.merriam-webster.com/dictionary/skill
[iii] "Outcome," *Merriam-Webster Dictionary*, Retrieved on March 17, 2013 from http://www.merriam-webster.com/dictionary/skill
[iv] Robert Penna, *The Nonprofit Outcomes Toolbox* (Hoboken: John Wiley & Sons, 2011), 19.

Terms in This Chapter

Investable Outcomes™

Outcomes presented from the investor's point of view, not the nonprofit's. Most importantly, an outcome worthy of a funder's money.

The Investment-Driven Model™ (IDM)

A process model for funding that builds on the components of *Asking Rights* and utilizes outcomes as the key to capitalize on investor motivations and leverage their investments.

NPO

Acronym for nonprofit organization.

CHAPTER 10

The Investment-Driven Model and Investable Outcomes

…nonprofit leaders are much more sophisticated about creating programs than they are about funding their organizations, and philanthropists often struggle to understand the impact (and limitations) of their donations.
- Ten Nonprofit Funding Models

MOVING BEYOND THE INGREDIENTS

The *Asking Rights* formula earns an organization the right and ability to successfully ask for money. It does not, however, guarantee that a funding campaign will be successful. If C+F+O are the necessary ingredients, the Investment-Driven Model (IDM) is the recipe. It's the process whereby the Credibility, Fundraising Skills, and Outcomes are combined to form a more successful funding effort. The IDM rose out of a need to boldly differentiate between the old-school fundraising model of purely emotional appeals and something fresh and more effective. After I introduced the concept of an "investment-based mindset" in *ROI for Nonprofits*, I quickly realized that "mindset" was not a strong enough word. It was a big step forward, but organizations were still not fully grasping certain concepts.

1. Value and impact could be the centerpiece of a fundraising strategy, not simply a collateral piece or a catch phrase.

2. The importance of outcomes and their value in the decision-making process of potential investors cannot be overstated.

3. Being able to answer an investor's question of "What's in it for me?" does not violate any mores in the fundraising process.

In the wake of *ROI for Nonprofits* release, as I traveled around the country doing lectures, workshops, and speaking engagements, what seemed to resonate most was the slide presented in Exhibit 10.1.

Exhibit 10.1 Presentation Slide

"If your organization doesn't demonstrate its value to potential funders, they'll fund an organization that does."

This one sentence was the salient point that most people remembered when they exited. It made sense, especially in the tight money recession.

Almost to a person they were experiencing some combination of budget shortfalls, unfulfilled pledges, and failed campaigns. And almost to a person they were relying on traditional methods of raising money. Why were these traditional methods falling short, time and time again? The answer, to me, was obvious.

How most nonprofit's approach fundraising can be summed up with one simple picture . . .

Yes, a tin cup. And all the implications that come with it: any amount of money is welcome, small change is fine, we just need a little, give something you won't miss, everyone is a target, etc. In a word, begging.

The bottom line of the IDM is to move a nonprofit from a charity with funding based to a large extent on begging to one of an organization worthy of bold investment. I have used the IDM model of fundraising — successfully — for the past 18 years. Over the years it has been tweaked, refined, and massaged, but never really fundamentally changed... because it works.

THE INVESTMENT-DRIVEN MODEL

Does the world need another business model? Of course not, but neither do we need another diet book or reality TV show. Thankfully, the IDM is not a business model; it is a completely new way of looking at how to raise money for nonprofits. It is a sustainable funding model, a better way to ensure consistent funding over the long term.

Fundamentally, the IDM is based on three patterns I observed during the successful execution of hundreds of campaigns.

1. Eliminating the gift mentality.
2. Emphasizing results.
3. Relying less on the emotional appeal.

121

These were termed "paradigm shifts" in *ROI for Nonprofits*, and this characterization still holds today. But there is more to it than shifting the paradigm. It really is a process.

The IDM's foundation lies in the following concepts introduced earlier in this book:

- The difference between a donor and an investor *(Chapters 1 and 2)*;

- The need for more than an emotional appeal *(Chapters 3 and 4)*; and

- The importance of the right metrics and demonstrating value *(Chapters 6 and 7)*.

It is also an extension of the logic model that had been a staple of nonprofits, especially in grant funding, which went beyond the program/output/outcome format to adding the value of those outcomes, which mean more in a fundraising situation.

The IDM gets to the heart of the matter. It is the process to fully monetize the characteristics of *Asking Rights*. Like the *Asking Rights* formula, the IDM is deceptively simple. At its most basic level, it only has four steps.

1. Discovering Investor Motivations
2. Translating Your Outcomes to Value
3. Matching Your Value to Investor Motivations
4. Using Campaign Dynamics to Maximize Funding

Step 1. Discovering Investor Motivations

If this step sounds familiar to a feasibility study, it is. It is one of the basic tenants of fundraising.

Before you ask someone for money, ask their opinion.

The IDM takes this thought and makes it more relevant to how money is raised for organizations in the 21st century by not relying exclusively on emotional appeals. It genuinely asks prospects, or potential investors, for their opinion and directs the discussion to how their opinion can be realized in tangible, non-emotional ways. The goal here is to discover what really interests them and what would motivate them to open their checkbooks, corporate or personal.

Business/Corporate Examples

- How might we position our program to make it more appealing to your marketing or business development efforts?

- How might your company benefit from the proposed program of work of this organization?

- Are there ways we could increase that benefit to you?

- Are there other sources of investment in your organization besides the philanthropic budget where our outcomes may be more valuable to you?

- How important is a tangible ROI to your giving program?

Personal/Family Examples

- Can we have your help in refining our outcomes so that they are more in line with your giving parameters or make more sense to other facets of your family's foundation's goals?

- Are you more interested in funding for operations, opportunities for facility improvements, or endowments for the future?

- Are your goals more immediate or more structural/long term?

- Is public recognition important to you?

- Do you have any ideas on how this organization can be more effective, ways that you might be interested in financially supporting?

After reading the above examples, imagine yourself in a meeting with a potential investor using an emotional appeal to try and extract information and uncover their motivations to invest. Tough, isn't it? And the more you try, the more you probably sound like a commercial or advertisement for your organization. Or you may find yourself using one of the better emotionally-based techniques, which is to lead with something that elicits an emotional reaction (usually negative), offer a solution/relief with something that prompts a positive emotional reaction, and invite the prospect to help you solve the problem/right the wrong/relieve the pain. However you do it, you are going to find that you are relying on advertising or sales types of techniques, rather than on discovering what is important to the potential investor. The feasibility stage is not for selling your program; it is the time to utilize those prized listening skills so that you can be open to hearing the critical evaluation of your project/goal/program, which will help to lead you to its success.

Another fundraising axiom is…

What they help write, they will help underwrite.

Some organizations have a problem with this. To these people, they feel that:

- It may make them look like they do not know what they are doing;

- They do not want outside interference in their programs;

- They do not want to feel like they are prostituting their mission or putting board seats up for sale or selling out to the highest bidder; and/or

- They are the experts and outsiders don't have a clue on what their organization should be focusing.

These are also the organizations that often have chronic funding problems.

Let's revisit Fundraising 101. By uncovering what potential investors are interested in, i.e. what motivates them to open their checkbook, we now have something with which to work. This is actually the second step of a two-step capital campaign process: first comes the feasibility study, then comes the campaign. Without knowing the feasibility of a campaign, there should never be a campaign. The study is the most important part of the entire process. If it is done incorrectly, campaigns take longer, are more expensive, and are more likely to be unsuccessful. Not only do studies uncover the landmines, they point the way for effective asks later on in an actual campaign. So often I've heard board members say, "We already know we need to raise money, so why do we need to spend money on a study to prove it?" A feasibility study doesn't prove that you need to raise money; it proves that you can—or cannot—raise the money you think you need (or sometimes think you deserve).

Step 2. Translating Your Outcomes to Value

Armed with the interests, motivations, and hot button issues of potential investors, it's now time to translate outcomes into examples that will make sense to prospects, putting the examples into a language they understand. Bankers, for instance, might like to see how their market share might increase. Service providers typically like to see how their customer base might grow. Wealthy individuals often like to see their legacy take the shape of a new building that is needed or an existing building in need of a name. Regular, middle class folks almost always like to see that a needed service to the community continues and thrives.

Translating outcomes into value can be done in many ways, some more quantitative than others. This is the step on which many nonprofits stumble, because they feel they don't have the necessary quantitative skills. Rather than learn the skills or hire outside assistance, they simply avoid the issue altogether, which is a costly mistake.

There are many translation to value techniques, including:

- Present value of future benefits;
- Cost savings;
- Opportunity costs;
- Net present value of the project;
- Multiplier effects;

- Positive benefits enhanced;
- Negative benefits reduced or eliminated;
- Delivery efficiencies; and
- The ubiquitous economic impact.

No matter how a value is reached, the important thing is that it has meaning to the potential investor. Bankers may have the very same motivations as area retirees, or they may be different, which is why Discovering Investor Motivations (Step 1) is so important.

Another common impediment to translating outcomes to value is that many nonprofits are need-based or internally focused, which isn't a bad thing when looking through an effectiveness or mission-based lens; it's just hard to raise money that way. By this I mean that their worldview goes something like this...

- Our needs are so great, how can someone not see that we need funding?
- The good work we do is so obvious, we don't need to explain it.
- If we focus on the program of work, the money will eventually materialize.
- How can someone not understand our value?
- If we build it, they will come.

To say that this way of thinking is naive is putting it mildly. Not only do the above views totally disregard the investor's point of view, they barely recognize the importance of demonstrating outcomes, much less the value of those outcomes. In today's world of competitive funding, failure by an organization to open its world view will likely lead to a shrinking budget and even less capacity to fulfill its mission.

Investable Outcomes

While not a substitute for the mathematics necessary to calculate value, a less quantitatively challenging method of "getting to value" is through what I call Investable Outcomes. Investable Outcomes are those worthy of a funder's dollars, and outcomes that are presented as community assets that are worthy of investment have a much better chance of being funded. Community, in this case, does not necessarily carry geographic connotations but can mean a group with similar interests. It is important to note that these are presented from the point of view of the investor, not the nonprofit!

Let's walk through an example in a logic model format to show the difference.

A health network and a hospital are being proactive in their decision to cooperatively build a new clinic to serve those not easily covered by health insurance. For the health network, it fulfills their mission to provide services to the poor, uninsured, and/or indigent. For the hospital, it helps prevent their emergency room from being clogged by being used as a primary care alternative, and allows care to be more geographically accessible. A proactive, win/win solution to the problem that is universally applauded in the community.

Output: Increased number of people that will now be able to receive preventative or urgent health care services. (This is the easily counted, very common "number of people served.")

Outcome: Fewer people sick because of preventative care, shorter recovery times, faster ER attention, and more efficient care delivery.

Value: Less time spent waiting for care, productivity not lost, fewer days of work missed, etc. (All are values that can be quantified in monetary terms.)

How do we make these outcomes Investable Outcomes? How do we put them in the investor's language and/or re-write them from the point of view of the investor? Let's keep going with our example to see.

This initiative is clearly being put forth by two organizations in the community with a proven ability to work well together and with respective expertise that, when combined, will meet an existing need in the community. The $1 million required to build the new facility is based on bids from local contractors. It will be managed by the health network and staffed by the hospital. The real estate has already been acquired; it is owned free and clear by the hospital. When operational, it will serve 50 people a day, six days a week, which equates to approximately 15,000 people per year. This will save an estimated 3,500 hours of lost productivity time per year in travel and waiting costs, and another 800 sick days per year because of preemptive/preventative treatment. The direct value of these savings is estimated to be more than $166,000 per year and the total impact of these efforts is projected to be more than $350,000 per year. An employer will likely realize a cost savings of $269 per worker per day in lost productivity avoided. The hospital will realize a 30 percent reduction in wait times, allowing for more cost effective staffing and lower emergency room charges.

What makes this project investable? Area employers are keenly aware of the disruption to production that can arise because of inadequate care for their workers. Other businesses understand that if people are missing work, maybe even losing their jobs because of the lack of access to medical care, that they will have less to spend on goods and services. Local leaders see that if they are able to keep the labor pool full, they can keep labor costs reasonable. Area residents will have a much better experience in the emergency room and their bills will likely be lower. In other words, this solution is one where the case can be crafted, to a large extent, on the benefits of self-interest. (Is that an audible gasp I hear?) Not once is there a need to mention how everyone will be healthy and happy, which is what an emotional appeal would do. An entire case can be built on the fact that this solution helps solve a problem, and the solution is valuable for both altruistic *and* self-interested investors.

A great example of how a program of work can be translated into Investable Outcomes is graphically illustrated in Exhibit 10.2. This example is taken from an annual Impact Report by Harbor House of Central Florida, an organization that seeks to eliminate domestic abuse.[i] It is chock full of outcomes on which the actual cost in dollars can be calculated, and presents those possibilities from various points of view, from co-workers to managers to the employer. It is a situation in which many businesses can easily relate, and sets the stage for successful funding.

Exhibit 10.2 Harbor House Investable Outcomes

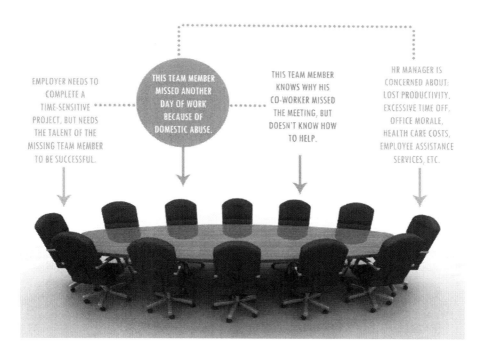

Simple Criteria

What is an Investable Outcome? It is an outcome that meets five criteria. It:

1. Passes the "reasonableness" test;
2. Has a likely chance of succeeding;

3. Provides an acceptable return on the required investment;

4. Allows the dots to be easily connected; and

5. Is valued by investors.

A bit more explanation on each below.

1. *Does it pass the "reasonableness" test?*

Is the desired outcome, or the plan to achieve it, reasonable, given the type of organization, its mission, size, etc.? While there is no universally definitive boundary as to when something becomes unreasonable, at this level, one of the goals is the avoidance of "sticker shock." In other words, is the price tag of the project/program of work reasonable, compared to the perceived value of the outcome delivered?

2. *Does it have a likely chance of succeeding?*

Is an organization capable of pulling this off? Can they do what they say they can? Do they have the expertise? Is it an area where they have succeeded before? When an organization enters into new markets, services, or is viewed as stretching their mission a bit too far, it sets off warning signals to potential investors.

3. *Does it provide an acceptable return on the required investment?*

Is the good that will be done by the investment commensurate with the amount of money being sought? Even though it might take some work, is it possible to calculate what the return might be in terms that matter to the investor? How long does the return take to materialize? Is there more upside than downside, or is the risk limited in any way?

4. *Does it allow the dots to be easily connected?*

Investors need to be shown, in plain language, how their investment will allow the project/initiative to succeed. In industry jargon, do the inputs logically lead to the outputs, which then lead to the outcomes? Can investors easily see that if a new program is introduced to the local arts organization, for example, it will lead to the outcome of the organization becoming financially sustainable as it is claiming?

5. *Is it valued by investors?*

This one is easy. Do the potential investors even care about this outcome? If the organization is viewed as one that provides local services, investors may not care that a new office will be opened 100 miles away. Is it something that investors will deem esoteric, not necessary, a stretch for the mission, or even frivolous?

Let's look at a few examples of real world Investable Outcomes and how they meet our criteria, presented from the potential investor's viewpoint.

Example #1 The amount of profit a local bank will realize on new deposits because of a growing local economy due to a $3 million economic development initiative.

1. *Does it pass the "reasonableness" test?*

It is reasonable to assume that if the economy grows, the bank will participate in that growth in that the project will attract new companies and a new workforce to the area, providing the bank with opportunities for new customers.

2. *Does it have a likely chance of succeeding?*

The nonprofit behind the effort has recruited companies to the area before.

3. *Does it provide an acceptable return on the required investment?*

The amount being sought for the project should result in three new companies locating to the area within 5 years, employing 800 people earning an average of $35,000 a year. Based on the bank's market share, a normal margin earned on deposit dollars, and a normal economy, the requested investment would seem acceptable.

4. *Does it allow the dots to be easily connected?*

Marketing the area leads to business relocation prospects, several of which will be enticed to relocate in the area if a good incentive package can be put together, which creates jobs, which creates demand for mortgages, car loans, checking accounts, etc.

5. *Is it valued by investors?*

A bank manager's goal is to grow his/her respective branch, which happens when the economy grows, and this initiative helps that to happen.

Example #2 It is much easier to recruit top corporate talent to the area because of the thriving arts/cultural organization in the community.

1. *Does it pass the "reasonableness" test?*

It is reasonable to assume that five years of new, quality exhibits will be appreciated by the type of people the community is trying to attract, and that they will be supporters of the organization. The $1.6 million being sought seems like enough to accomplish that goal.

2. *Does it have a likely chance of succeeding?*

The arts/culture organization has the reputation, the leadership, and the track record of bringing exhibits to town that are very popular.

3. *Does it provide an acceptable return on the required investment?*

The amount of project money being sought should help attract 8,000 new visitors per year and allow membership to increase 20 percent. More than half of the new visitors will be from outside the area, which will also help the restaurants and hotels in the area. The initiative goal seems like a bargain for these types of returns on investment.

4. *Does it allow the dots to be easily connected?*

New exhibits will lead to new visitors and increased visitation will allow the organization to be much more visible and viable. This visibility will allow the reputation of the area to grow as a regional cultural center.

5. *Is it valued by investors?*

> The goal of local businesses is to grow, which requires continual effort to attract top talent, who tend to value the arts and other cultural amenities. This project ensures that arts and culture activities remain viable, thus helping to recruit talent to the area.

Example #3 Keeping kids busy in organized sports activities helps to keep them from becoming delinquents, and is more cost effective than paying higher taxes to subsidize law enforcement, judicial, and incarceration efforts.

1. *Does it pass the "reasonableness" test?*

> It is reasonable to assume that a facility dedicated to organized youth sports would allow kids a productive outlet for their energy and keep them from roaming the street looking for trouble. The $4.8 million being sought seems reasonable to build the structure and staff the facility.

2. *Does it have a likely chance of succeeding?*

> The organization wanting to build the new facility operates several similar facilities in the area, and they feel that they can manage another one successfully.

3. *Does it provide an acceptable return on the required investment?*

> While the costs associated with the organization's program of work may be high, the costs of the negative outcomes associated with not funding the project are higher. The facility will serve an average of 200 kids per year, and the value of lower crime costs, a safer neighborhood and, most importantly, positive outcomes for the kids, make this a solid investment.

4. *Does it allow the dots to be easily connected?*

> A program that encourages and supervises kids in a positive way, and at the same time minimizes the negative, criminal activities in the area, is a no brainer. The facility and staff to implement the program are needed.

5. *Is it valued by investors?*

> People want to improve their community and make their neighborhoods safe. Doing so creates an inviting situation for young families, increases property values, encourages community involvement and reduces crime. These are all things that people value in their community.

To be sure, many of the steps in the previous examples will take a lot of work to connect the dots and demonstrate ROI, but the steps are an accurate depiction of how outcomes can be transformed into Investable Outcomes.

When outcomes are approached from the perspective of these five steps, they gain much more traction with potential investors, resulting in shorter campaigns, larger investments, and more dollars raised.

Step 3. Matching Your Value to Investor Motivations

Whereas in the first step we discovered what a potential investor values, in this step we are armed with outcomes *that we already know will be important to them*! It is a no-fail proposition... if executed correctly. It's like the old axiom of how to make a presentation:

1. Tell'em what you are going to tell'em;

2. Tell'em; and then

3. Tell'em what you told'em.

This third step is more of the deliberate process of getting in front of potential investors and presenting them with something that is meaningful to them. It is a vitally important step often overlooked by those who constantly think "if we only had the magic ROI number," the money would just flow into the nonprofit. Organizations that think this way seem to be enamored with the concept of nonprofit ROI, but place too much emphasis on the mechanics of it and not nearly enough on the communication of it. They love the "how" but neglect the "why."

As a 2009 article in the *Stanford Social Innovation Review* states, "When nonprofits and funding sources are not well matched, money doesn't flow to the areas where it will do the greatest good. Too often, the result is that promising programs are cut, curtailed, or never launched. And when dollars become tight, a chaotic scramble is all the more likely to ensue."[ii] In one sense, a campaign can be viewed as a matching exercise. The NPO has outcomes and the work is not in changing the outcomes to fit investors, but to find investors that value your outcomes. This is a process I call Letting Outcomes Drive.

Letting Outcomes Drive

Letting Outcomes Drive has a double meaning. First, it reinforces the fact that outcomes can be the driver of a funding *strategy*. Second, it says that outcomes really are in charge of driving the funding *vehicle* (capital campaign, annual campaign, ongoing fund development, etc.), much like the driver is in charge of the car.

These truths are in stark contrast to how many nonprofits approach a major campaign. When nonprofits hear that I am based in Atlanta, they naturally assume that I can help them get money from Coca Cola, United Parcel Service, Home Depot, and any number of Fortune 500 entities that are headquartered or have large operations here. Unfortunately, proximity does not trump process. On a more localized level, when the list of prospects is developed at the beginning of a campaign, the NPO typically lists the usual, deep-pocketed suspects first. I have even heard this comment, said with complete sincerity, "One of the people about a mile down the road knows Oprah." The correct approach is 180 degrees from this type of thinking.

There are two much more effective ways to view the interplay of outcomes and investors.

1. Use the Motivational Pyramid first put forth by Kay Sprinkle Grace in *Beyond Fundraising*, where the categories of Connection, Concern, and Capacity offer guidelines. (See Exhibit 6.1) Whereas most NPOs start at the bottom and work up, they should start at the top and work down. In other words, start with those people most connected to the organization and its outcomes, not those with simply the

capacity to stroke a check but no connection to the organization.

2. Letting Outcomes Drive is the process of first making your outcomes completely clear, then matching them to those most likely to value them. Even better? Match outcomes with those who benefit most from your efforts.

For example, if one of your outcomes is that you provide training so people can enter the work force with a higher level of skill, then the outcome should point you to those employers that benefit from your efforts. Approaching them in a fundraising context will also provide interaction that could lead to some interesting partnerships. On a more macro level, if you are saving the taxpayers money by reducing crime through positive youth services and activities, then you are letting your outcomes drive you to a broad audience. Leveraging outcomes, the positive impact on your primary customers, with supporting customers, whose money makes this possible, is a win/win for which many nonprofits strive.

Step 4. Using Campaign Dynamics to Maximize Funding

Campaign dynamics encompass more than simply making the ask. They include the management of a campaign and effectively capture the interaction of people engaged in one synergistic effort.

So, what are campaign dynamics?

Peer-to-peer leverage
In a nod to traditional fundraising, peer-to-peer leverage is very valuable. Traditional fundraisers would define peer-to-peer leverage as utilizing the more senior/influential volunteer as the primary "asker" for investment. Personally, I define it differently. While the presence of a senior/influential volunteer in the room is important, I do not put them in the position of asking their friends and business associates for money, risking personal and/or professional relationships. The old adage "people give to people" implies that if the prospect knows the asker, then the odds of success are higher. I cannot argue with this, but you have to have

more than familiarity. Credibility and Outcomes are still necessary.

Peer-to-peer leverage involves…

- Not only knowledge of the other person, but the presence of some level of personal or professional respect. Common sense tells you that if the prospect does not personally or professionally respect the person involved in the ask, then there really is no leverage present.

- Leverage implies that the asker has already made their investment. If the asker has not already done this, it screams of hypocrisy and the ask will not be successful.

Calibration to leaders

No matter how big or how small the community, city, or region, it is human nature to compare what you may be asked to invest with what others are being asked to invest. With banks, for example, it is relatively easy to determine that one bank may be five times larger than the other. It is not unusual, then, that the smaller bank may ask what the larger bank is investing.

There are, of course, extenuating circumstances. One bank or banker may want to make a big splash on a particular initiative for professional or personal reasons. Or on an individual level, one person may feel that another person has twice as much wealth and therefore should invest twice as much.

The important point is that calibration happens, regardless of whether it's the most professional way to do things or not. The impact on a campaign can be huge; if the very top leadership is not at the level they need to be, say 15 percent of the total goal, then when everybody calibrates to them, the investments in total will undoubtedly fall short of the goal. This is why evaluation skills and the ability to make the correct ask are so important.

Sequential asks: Top down, inside out process

This is also one of those Fundraising 101 tactics often touted but largely ignored. Similar to the motivation pyramid of Kay Sprinkle Grace, sequential asks guide a campaign to start with the top prospects and go down the list while simultaneously beginning with the people closest to the organization and moving out to those less connected.

Violating this rule can have disastrous consequences, because if you think the people you are targeting don't talk to each other or know what's going on, you are fooling only yourself. Prospects will offer questions such as, "Why are you asking me for $100,000 when Bob, who sits on your board and has a lot more money than me, is only in for $10,000?" (In case you missed it, see *Calibration to leaders*).

Ownership: Their campaign, not yours

At the end of the day, the campaign belongs to the NPO, not to the campaign consultant or even to the investors. Making this point completely and unequivocally understood by the NPO is essential to the initiative's success. Without ownership, the NPO becomes distant from the day-to-day campaign dynamics, missing the opportunity to provide critical input in a timely manner and to gain valuable insight on the community and its leadership, which could be useful during and after the campaign. No matter how talented the outside fundraising counsel may be, and no matter how much money they help to raise, it is still not their campaign.

It is said that success has many fathers, but failure is an orphan. Organizational ownership of a fundraising effort is a great example of this. When campaigns get off track, the NPO must be involved in getting it back on track. And when a campaign succeeds, the NPO should get all of the credit. Outside counsel should be invisible in this respect.

In this chapter we have introduced a lot of new concepts, including the IDM and Investable Outcomes as the next steps to monetizing the ingredients of *Asking Rights*. The next chapter continues the discussion on how the IDM shares the traits of broader management models, and why it has proven to be so successful.

REFERENCES

[i] "Impact Report 2011-2012," Harbor House of Central Florida, 12.
[ii] William Landes Foster, Barbara Christiansen and Kim Peter, "Ten Nonprofit Funding Models," *Stanford Social Innovation Review* (Spring 2010): 32.

CHAPTER 11

Driving the IDM Further

In the for-profit world, companies live or die by
whether they're getting better at what they deliver, and
in the nonprofit world, we need to be doing the same.
- *Elisabeth Babcock*

ONE MORE CATEGORY

As established in the last chapter, the IDM is a process model, not a business model.

The lack of nonprofit process models—funding models in particular—is what caused Foster et al to write *Ten Nonprofit Funding Models*, a paper that originally appeared in the Spring 2009 *Stanford Social Innovation Review*[i]. Especially valuable is the part where models are described.

> "…the critical aspects (and accompanying vocabulary) of nonprofit funding models need to be understood separately from those of the for-profit world. It is also why we use the term *funding model* rather than *business model* to describe the framework. A business model incorporates choices about the cost structure and value proposition to the beneficiary. A funding model, however, focuses only on the funding, not on the programs and services offered to the beneficiary."

One point made in an early section is the "financial fuzziness" of the lexicon used in the nonprofit world. In the for-profit world, when a company says it's a "low-cost provider," everyone instantly understands quite a bit about the business model. The same would hold for other model descriptions and categories, such as "multi-level marketing," "franchisor," or "razor and the razor blade." The last term, I feel I can confidently say, is more easily understood in present times by the phrase "printer and printer ink cartridge," whereby once the initial product is purchased, often very inexpensively, it virtually ensures many more purchases in the future. These future purchases often have much higher margins to the producer than the original product.

The paper's research focused on three parameters to ultimately define the funding models: the source of the funds, the types of decision makers, and the motivations of the decision makers. All are vitally important pieces of information, and all fit very well into the discussion of moving beyond a model to the process of actually raising money.

The Ten Funding Models are presented in Exhibit 11.1 with enough detail so that some relevant conclusions—as they relate to both the *Asking Rights* formula and the IDM—can be drawn.

Exhibit 11.1 Ten Funding Models

Model Name	Funding Source	Funding Decision Maker	Funding Motivation
1. Heartfelt Connector	Individual	Multitude of Individuals	Altruism
2. Beneficiary Builder	Individual	Multitude of Individuals	Self-Interest or Altruism
3. Member Motivator	Individual	Multitude of Individuals	Collective Interest
4. Big Bettor	Individual or Foundation	Few individuals	Altruism
5. Public Provider	Government	Administrators	Collective Interest
6. Policy Innovator	Government	Policy Makers	Collective Interest
7. Beneficiary Broker	Government	Multitude of Individuals	Self-Interest
8. Resource Recycler	Corporate	Few Individuals	Self-Interest
9. Market Maker	Mixed	Mass or Few Individuals	Altruism or Self-Interest
10. Local Nationalizer	Mixed	Few Individuals	Altruism

Here are some important points to note.

1. Even though the Funding Source may be listed as Individual, it does not preclude Corporations from playing a major role in the funding process.

2. This study included nonprofits but excluded hospitals and universities founded since 1970 that had reached $50 million in annual revenue. The result was a pool of 144 organizations.

3. While this study focused on larger NPOs, some of the conclusions are important for smaller nonprofits. In a subsequent article in the *Stanford Social Innovation Review*, the

study's authors suggest that these lessons are applicable when a nonprofit reaches $3 million in annual revenues.[ii]

How does this research relate to *Asking Rights*/the IDM?

1. *It validates that matching outcomes to funding sources can be the strategy to fast growth.* One of the more interesting conclusions of this work is that the organizations studied "…got big not by diversifying their funding sources, but by raising their money from a single type of funding (such as corporations or government) that was a natural match for their mission."

2. *Motivation matters.* The simple fact that the authors chose to use motivation as a determining/descriptive category in their research speaks volumes of its importance.

3. *Self-interest as a motivator works.* Altruism as a funding motivation was listed three times and self-interest twice. Okay, so altruism wins by a nose. While it is not fair to equate altruism solely with emotional appeals and self-interest solely with rational appeals, since a person can be very emotional about his/her own self-interest, experience has shown that rational appeals work very well with the self-interest crowd. When self-interest is combined with collective interest motivations and those with multiple motivations, the count reaches seven out of ten. What better way to monetize the motivations of those with personal or collective interests than to show them "What's in it for me?"

At the risk of comparing rigorous research to experience, let me offer Exhibit 11.2, in which I have added "Outcome Deliverer" as one more model to the original list of 10.

Exhibit 11.2 An 11th Category

	Model Name	Funding Source	Funding Decision Maker	Funding Motivation
1.	Heartfelt Connector	Individual	Multitude of Individuals	Altruism
2.	Beneficiary Builder	Individual	Multitude of Individuals	Self-Interest or Altruism
3.	Member Motivator	Individual	Multitude of Individuals	Collective Interest
4.	Big Bettor	Individual or Foundation	Few individuals	Altruism
5.	Public Provider	Government	Administrators	Collective Interest
6.	Policy Innovator	Government	Policy Makers	Collective Interest
7.	Beneficiary Broker	Government	Multitude of Individuals	Self-Interest
8.	Resource Recycler	Corporate	Few Individuals	Self-Interest
9.	Market Maker	Mixed	Mass or Few Individuals	Altruism or Self-Interest
10.	Local Nationalizer	Mixed	Few Individuals	Altruism
11.	**Outcome Deliverer**	**Individual, Corporate, and/or Foundation**	**Few Individuals**	**Self-Interest and/or Collective-Interest**

Much of my experience and success has been working with organizations with budgets of $10 million or less, and I have seen time and again that a focus on delivering outcomes is a strategy that cuts across the funding source, the funding decision maker, and the funding motivation. In fact, it may work better for these smaller nonprofits because the process of matching outcomes to funders who appreciate them is more manageable.

THE MBO/FBO COMPARISON

One of Peter Drucker's more widely known theories is *management by objectives* (MBO), a process whereby objectives are mutually defined by both management and employee so that everyone understands what needs to be done to successfully reach the stated goals. The term "management by objectives" was first popularized in his 1954 book *The Practice of Management*.

Let's look at some of the important characteristics of MBO.

1. Motivation – MBO involves employees, not just management, in the entire process of goal setting, since people will tend to have a higher commitment to objectives they set for themselves than those imposed on them by management.

2. Better Results – This involvement in goal setting increases employee job satisfaction and commitment.

144

3. Better Overall Management – Managers are better able to ensure that employees' objectives are linked to the organization's overall objectives.

4. Clarity – Since everyone, both employees and management, were involved in setting the goals and objectives, it is clear to all involved what needs to be done to be successful.

Funding By Objectives

The parallels between MBO concepts and a feasibility study, the first step in a funding campaign, are both obvious and startling. A feasibility studies involves:

- Mutual goal setting;
- Uncovering the motivations of those involved;
- Determining a realistic goal; and
- A path to success involving both funders and those being funded.

In a turn of phrase, MBO—when overlaid in the nonprofit funding arena—becomes Funding by Objectives, which leads to a more successful campaign as a result. Perhaps Funding by *Outcomes*, rather than Objectives, is even more appropriate given the focus on outcomes we have emphasized in *Asking Rights*.

Campaign Management

One of the more notable detractors of MBO was noted management theory pioneer W. Edwards Deming, who argued that "a lack of understanding of systems commonly results in the misapplication of objectives." He also argued that setting production targets will encourage the reaching of those targets through whatever means necessary, which usually results in poor quality.[iii] Another of his criticisms of MBO was that "it over-emphasizes the setting of goals over the working of a plan as a driver of outcomes."[iv]

Let's apply Deming's concerns of too much emphasis on the objectives themselves, rather than the work plan to reach those objectives, to Funding by Outcomes. This is what actively managing a campaign is all about. Setting the financial goal of the campaign, while involving many details, is the easy part. The hard work is in opening doors, scheduling appointments, presenting a customized value proposition, making the ask, following up, making the ask again, following up, and so on. If not done correctly, a poor quality campaign will result.

SAME IDEA, DIFFERENT WORDS?

As discussed previously, a pivotal part of the IDM is developing Investable Outcomes. Nonprofits have long acknowledged the importance of outcomes on their primary customers from an operations, strategy, and management perspective, but making them mean something to fundraising targets is easier said than done. Using outcomes in a fundraising context seems to have hit a new level of popularity, as evidenced by Jason Saul in his book *The End of Fundraising*.

> "In recent years, consultants and fundraisers have encouraged nonprofits to be 'outcome-driven,' and focus on results to increase their appeal to funders. That's certainly better than the opposite. But that's only half of the story. It's not just about producing an outcome; it's about producing high-value outcomes. The fact is, not all outcomes are created equal … It turns out that there are different levels of outcomes - *degrees of impact* - some of which carry greater currency in the social capital market than others."[v]

I obviously agree with the fact that those of us in the business of raising money have encouraged this, and can't help but feel he was speaking directly to me when he wrote the above words (Note: "OutcomeDrivenConsulting.com" is one of Convergent Nonprofit Solutions' web addresses). Nonprofit investors brought up the fact that some outcomes carry more weight than others years ago. We had to listen or they would not invest. Saul's three types of "high-value outcomes" — change in status or condition, ROI, and systemic change — are a good way to categorize and think about the outcomes produced by one's organization, and we both fundamentally agree on how important outcomes are in the funding strategy.

His view of the future of nonprofit funding describes those most likely to invest in an NPO as *impact buyers,* and he splits those buyers into five categories: service providers, upstream consumers, corporate partners, beneficiaries that can pay, and social investors. Since these are typical prospects in a fundraising campaign, he and I also fundamentally agree on these funder categories.

Where we diverge are the ideas of *selling* and *buying* impact, and analyzing impact versus raising money. I initially thought our difference of opinion was small, maybe just semantics, until I read this:

> "I have measured the outcomes of thousands of nonprofit organizations, and analyzed the impact of over $950 million in funding."[vi]

Measuring outcomes or analyzing impact as an academic or quantitative exercise can certainly shed some light on the debate, but they are not the same as actually raising money. If I was *selling* anything, I don't feel the funding efforts would have been nearly as successful. I don't consider funding prospects to be *buyers:* I consider them investors.

Approaching prospects as buyers and needing to "sell" them something casts the process of a fundraising campaign in a simplistic and somewhat seedy light. It also seems to disregard many of the tools necessary in the fundraising trenches, i.e. the campaign dynamics needed so the effort is cohesive and builds momentum versus a series of isolated selling attempts.

WHY IS THE IDM SO SUCESSFUL?

As a summary to the discussion of the IDM, let me share with you the reasons why it is such a successful fundraising model:

1. *It focuses on the decision maker.*
    This is exactly where any fundraising solicitation should be focused.

2. *It positions the organization as a community asset.*
   Assets are considered more permanent than programs and have long-term benefits.

3. *It utilizes outcomes that are investable.*
   Some outcomes are better than others.

4. *It is presented in a language that the investor can relate to and can easily understand.*
   Nobody invests in something they do not understand.

5. *It addresses the motivation to invest.*
   This is rationally-based and results in more dollars raised.

REFERENCES

[i] Peter Kim, Gail Perreault, and William Foster, "Finding Your Funding Model," *Stanford Social Innovation Review* (Fall 2011), Retrieved on March 17, 2013, from http://www.ssireview.org/articles/entry/finding_your_funding_model
[ii] Ibid.
[iii] Ibid.
[iv] "Management by Objectives," *Wikipedia,* Retrieved March 17, 2013, from http://en.wikipedia.org/wiki/Management_by_objectives
[v] Jason Saul, *The End of Fundraising* (San Francisco: Jossey-Bass, 2001), 115.
[vi] Ibid, 117.

CHAPTER 12

Do You Have Asking Rights?
Results from workshops and seminars

Asking Rights must be earned and must be constantly
cultivated. Your organization doesn't have them just
because you exist.
                                        - Bob Johnson

I DON'T WANT YOU TO HIRE ME

At first blush, the answer to the question "Do you have *Asking
Rights*?" may seem pretty straightforward. If you read the previous
chapters, you now know that if you have the C, the F, and the O,
then you do. But, as with most things in life, it's not always that
simple.

Several years before the patterns emerged that allowed certain traits
to be distilled into a formula, when the ROI/rational/what's-in-it-
for-me approach was more of an oddity, say 2005 or so, my
company would get a lot of inquiries from nonprofits about our
services. Often our services were just not a good fit, but being a
small shop always looking to grow, it was not in my DNA to turn
them away. The mere thought of turning down a potential client
was unnatural, and I was not personally good at it, even though I
intellectually knew that:

- We may not be able to help them;
- They were not ready for the services we offered;
- They were not a good fit for my company;
- They had some work to do before anyone could help them;

- The amount of time involved would make it an unprofitable proposition; and/or
- They expected miracles.

My solution was to provide them with a set of self-assessment questions, letting them determine if their goals and our methods were a good fit. Depending on their answers, I would welcome the continuation of the conversation of working together towards their success.

Since the *Asking Rights* concept was already firmly in my vernacular, I decided that a "Do You Have *Asking Rights*?" quiz would serve dual purposes.

1. It would give nonprofits a good idea of how my firm approached things, including the vocabulary I use, and what I considered important to attract major funders.

2. It was an easy way to see how they assessed themselves, so I could more easily tell them that they A) would be a good fit for our firm, B) had some homework to do before taking on a major fundraising initiative, or C) might be better suited for a different fundraising firm.

After some tweaking, the format that emerged is shown on the following pages. It was designed not only to be something that I could email to a prospect to qualify them as a client, but something that I could use during my workshops and seminars as an on-screen tool. Only later did I actually make it a worksheet that was collected for analysis purposes.

Does your NPO have "Asking Rights" for major funding?
Here are the 20 key questions we use to assess if your
organization can attract major investors.

DEFINE YOUR MODEL

1. Is demand for your services growing faster than your revenue?
   ☐ Yes   ☐ No

2. Do you consider employee turnover to be low?
   ☐ Yes   ☐ No

3. Is your strategic plan a document that is referred to often?
   ☐ Yes   ☐ No

4. Do you know how much funding you will need over the next three years?
   ☐ Yes   ☐ No

5. Is over half your annual budget from sources that will expire in less than three years?
   ☐ Yes   ☐ No

UNDERSTAND YOUR INVESTORS

6. Do fees for services make up more than 30% of annual revenue?
   ☐ Yes   ☐ No

7. Do board members make almost all of your meetings?
   ☐ Yes   ☐ No

8. Is there a waiting list for your board?
   ☐ Yes   ☐ No

9. Does more than 50% of your budget come from grants?
   ☐ Yes   ☐ No

10. Could you increase your dues/fees by 100% without losing more than 50% your members?
   ☐ Yes   ☐ No

UNDERSTAND YOUR OUTCOMES

11. Do your outcomes relate easily to your funders?

☐ Yes ☐ No

12. Do you regularly communicate the value of your outcomes?

☐ Yes ☐ No

13. Do your outcomes create an acceptable level of ROI to investors?

☐ Yes ☐ No

14. Are your outcomes easily understood by your constituency?

☐ Yes ☐ No

15. Are funders investing in your outcomes rather than your organization?

☐ Yes ☐ No

ESTABLISH ASKING RIGHTS

16. Is your largest funding source more than 10% of your budget?

☐ Yes ☐ No

17. Do you generally achieve your annual goals/objectives?

☐ Yes ☐ No

18. Was your last funding effort over goal?

☐ Yes ☐ No

19. Have you been established for five or more years?

☐ Yes ☐ No

20. Are board members major investors in your organization?

☐ Yes ☐ No

THE METHOD TO THE MADNESS

Obviously, this quiz was not appropriate for every workshop, conference, seminar, or even every client. My best guess is that approximately 800 people or so saw it as part of a presentation during the course of four years. It was designed to be quick, understandable without much explanation, and easy to score in a group setting.

The basic ideas behind each section and question are explained below to give some insight into the purpose behind the process.

DEFINE YOUR MODEL

This section was designed to quickly determine how the community might perceive the organization in terms of model characteristics: growth, financing needs, planning, etc. It also helps to answer "What type of shop do you run?"

Question #1
Is the demand for your services growing faster than your revenue?

Answer Reveals:

Is their particular service in high demand? Is there a sense of urgency (which helps when fundraising)? Is there actually any funding at all?

Question #2
Do you consider employee turnover to be low?

Answer Reveals:

Do people want to work for this organization? Is a stable management team in place? Are there structural obstacles, such as low pay, that take attention away from the mission of the organization?

Question #3
Is your strategic plan a document that is referred to often?

Answer Reveals:

Is the organization forward thinking? Is there a strategic plan? Is it a massive binder that sits on a shelf collecting dust or is it manageable and achievable? Is there an appreciation for good management tools or are they just going through the motions?

Question #4
Do you know how much funding you will need over the next 3 years?

Answer Reveals:

Are plans well thought through enough to have price tags on them? This question relates to the previous one in that knowing what you want to do is one thing, but knowing how you will pay for it is a different matter entirely.

Question #5
Is over half your annual budget from sources that will expire in less than 3 years?

Answer Reveals:

How financially at risk is the organization? How stable are existing funding sources? Is the business model nothing but a continual search for funding?

UNDERSTAND YOUR INVESTORS

This section deals with the board, a group of people who are usually steady investors in an organization, and the other major sources of funding. Grants and dues are addressed specifically, since many organizations rely on those particular sources.

Question #6
Do fees for services make up more than 30% of annual revenue?

Answer Reveals:

How financially sustainable is the organization? Is there a revenue stream that indicates self-sufficiency? Investors typically like to see some sort of organically-based revenue, even if it's relatively small in the total funding portfolio.

Question #7
Do board members make almost all of your meetings?

Answer Reveals:

How involved is the board? Is there a leadership problem or, worse, a leadership vacuum? Are meetings effective?

Question #8

Is there a waiting list for your board?

Answer Reveals:

How popular is the organization within its own community? Is this the board that everyone wants to be on? A waiting list implies all of the right things in terms of future fundraising.

Question #9

Does more than 50% of your budget come from grants?

Answer Reveals:

This question had a very specific purpose: is funding overly dependent on one source? Often times, those that answered "yes" were those organizations that received more than 50 percent of their funding from one single source... the federal government. Remember, the goal is to establish whether the organization has what it takes to attract major investors, and a dependence on federal money is normally a deterrent.

Question #10

Could you increase your dues/fees by 100% without losing more than 50% of your members?

Answer Reveals:

What does the demand curve look like for services? Is the service highly price sensitive? How many other NPOs offer similar services?

UNDERSTAND YOUR OUTCOMES

It should be no surprise that, since *Asking Rights* depend so heavily on outcomes, this section is very important. How outcomes are communicated, their ROI, and the effectiveness of the organization's investor relations program are all critical to success and need to be examined.

Question #11

Do your outcomes relate easily to your funders?

Answer Reveals:

Most respondents naturally answered "yes" to this question, which was not surprising. The goal was to get them thinking that outcomes and funding are related. A "no" response might indicate an overly complicated situation or one that is under the radar of most funders.

Question #12
Do you regularly communicate the value of your outcomes?

Answer Reveals:
> Are investor relations a priority? Is there the ability and capacity to value outcomes?

Question #13
Do your outcomes create an acceptable level of ROI to investors?

Answer Reveals:
> This is probably the most complicated question of the entire quiz. If funding was on the decline, it might indicate that an acceptable level of ROI was not being generated. It also sparks the discussion of how to actually calculate ROI, not just use the acronym in a generic sense.

Question #14
Are your outcomes easily understood by your constituency?

Answer Reveals:
> This answer should parallel the answer to #11, and was designed to be a check question. The word *constituency* is broader in scope than *funders*, and for many this is more indicative of general marketing or brand than of fundraising.

Question #15
Are funders investing in your outcomes rather than your organization?

Answer Reveals:
> This question was often a prelude to the content of the workshop or seminar. While it is possible that funders will invest because of the credibility of the organization, many NPOs don't have this broad-based credibility. In such cases, the campaign shifts to raising money on outcomes, since reputation alone is not usually enough for large funding infusions.

ESTABLISH ASKING RIGHTS

This section deals directly with the topic *Asking Rights*, and by this point respondents normally see the correlation of a positive response and a higher score.

Question #16

Is your largest funding source more than 10% of your budget?

Answer Reveals:

While similar to earlier questions about fees for services (#6) and grants (#9), this question has more to do with the diversification of the total funding portfolio. When one source of funding accounts for a large portion of the total funding, it can help in establishing *Asking Rights* because credibility is present.

Question #17

Do you generally achieve your annual goals/objectives?

Answer Reveals:

Again, an affirmative answer would equate to better *Asking Rights*. People want to invest in successful organizations.

Question #18

Was your last funding effort over goal?

Answer Reveals:

Has the organization been out there in the fundraising trenches? How much was raised? If the goal wasn't reached, are there solid reasons why?

Question #19

Have you been established for 5 or more years?

Answer Reveals:

This question goes to stability, track record, and general place in the community. New organizations typically have a tougher road ahead of them when competing with those NPOs that are well established.

Question #20
Are board members major investors in your organization?

Answer Reveals:

It is very difficult to ask others who are not as close to the organization to invest when those who are closest are not investors themselves. Not impossible, but more difficult.

SOME QUANTITATIVE EVIDENCE

Even though this quiz is useful as a workshop tool to stimulate discussion, I soon realized that some hard data would aid the effort. The following table lists the variety of sizes and shapes of groups where questionnaires were collected. The scoring was simple: one point for each "yes" response. It was designed so that organizations that had previously been successful in attracting new investors would normally score well above 15 points.

Scores were categorized into three groups.

1. **Ready to Roll** – An organization that answered "yes" *more than 15 times* has *Asking Rights* and is well positioned to attract major investors.

2. **Homework to Do** – An organization that answered "yes" *5 to 15 times* still has some preliminary work to do before any major funding effort is launched.

3. **Do Not Attempt** – An organization that answered "yes" *less than 5 times* is in a funding vacuum and organizational growth will likely be severely limited in the near term.

Type of Group	Number in Group	Average Score	Standard Deviation
Community Foundation Workshop Series	6	12.7	1.63
National Grantee Workshop	10	12.4	2.22
Statewide Conference	22	10.0	2.98
Community Foundation Workshop	32	10.3	2.68
Private Foundation Workshop Series	12	11.0	2.98
Statewide Grantee Workshop	19	12.9	1.70
Statewide Conference	22	13.8	1.57
Statewide Grantee Workshop	12	11.5	2.28
National Conference	78	12.0	2.67

Group Averages

Average Group Score	11.84
Standard Deviation of Group Scores	1.24

Total Sample

Total Number	213
Average Score	11.76
Standard Deviation Total Sample	2.70
High Score	19
Low Score	5

WHAT THIS TOLD US

The short answer is that the average group and the groups as a whole still had some work to do to be successful in attracting major investors. This was to be expected, since the sample was somewhat self-selective in that they were all attending a program to learn something about nonprofit ROI, how to relate outcomes to funding, or financial sustainability.

Some specifics of the sampling include:

- Group scores were fairly consistent across size *and* geography;
- Scores varied widely, with the highest score at 19 and the lowest at 5; and

- The highest scoring section was Understand Your Outcomes, where it was not uncommon for people to answer "yes" to all five questions.

A deeper look at individual answers yielded some interesting patterns as well. Six questions emerged that seemed to naturally group together, with each of them at more than 83 percent answering "yes." Two questions were also grouped together with "no" responses, each at more than an 85 percent response rate.

The top six questions with the most "yes" responses, in order, were:

1. *Is your largest funding source more than 10% of your budget?* (#16)

2. *Do you generally achieve your annual goals/objectives?* (#17)

3. *Is the demand for your services growing faster than your revenue?* (#1)

4. *Do your outcomes relate easily to your funders?* (#11)

5. *Do you consider employee turnover to be low?* (#2)

6. *Does more than 50% of your budget come from grants?* (#9)

The top two questions with the most "no" responses, in order, were:

1. *Is there a waiting list for your board?* (#8)

2. *Do fees for services make up more than 30% of annual revenue?* (#6)

Using the individual responses, the typical profile of the organization in the sample:

- Is heavily dependent on grant funding;
- Is generally successful in reaching their objectives;
- Runs a stable operation;
- Provides services that are in demand; and
- Has some board development work to do.

The dependence on grant funding was no surprise, given the types of groups included in the sample. Since most of the grantees I have met tend to feel they do a good job in fulfilling the requirements of their respective grants, these responses were also not a surprise.

Now let me add some more information. Approximately half of the sample did not achieve their last funding goal, had not yet been around for five years, and had board members who were not investors in their organization. The top "no" answer, at 91 percent, was that there was no waiting list for their board. Adding these characteristics to the fact that the average organization had a score of 12, meaning that they still had some work to do before earning *Asking Rights*, I was able to reach a few conclusions.

These organizations:

- Are operating somewhat under the radar in their communities;
- Are too new to establish real credibility;
- Have a board that is not leading the way with its own dollars;
- Are lacking in fundraising skills; and
- Believe that their outcomes are valuable.

This paints the picture of stable yet unexciting organizations that are in constant search of the next grant. In their current state, they would have a difficult time raising money from new sources and definitely have some homework to do before any attempt at such an undertaking. The 20 questions do exactly what they are intended to do: help determine if an organization has the raw material to attract new investors and, by and large, this set did not. This exercise opened some eyes, and those attending these workshops expressed their appreciation.

Bob Johnson, a colleague of mine at Convergent Nonprofit Solutions, developed a well-thought-out list several years ago that he left with clients at the conclusion of a project. He implored his clients to develop their own *Asking Rights* by having them ask themselves a series of eight questions.

Do you:

1. Provide a meaningful service?
2. Operate in an efficient, cost-effective manner?
3. Frequently tell your audience how you spend their investment?
4. Collaborate, and when possible, seek suggestions and other viewpoints?
5. Achieve relevant, meaningful, and planned-for results?
6. Meet the needs of supporters, potential or actual?
7. Communicate with your audience... clearly, concisely, and continuously?
8. Consistently and personally express appreciation to investors and friends?

To this list, one could also easily add "Operate ethically?" and "Use the services and products of your constituency whenever possible?" Bob's list and my approach of C+F+O aim at the same goal: ensuring organizations understand and correctly employ *Asking Rights* so that they can succeed in not just their funding campaigns, but in their missions.

The original *Asking Rights* quiz of 20 questions certainly provided some important insights into how nonprofits viewed themselves. It had a strong flavor of budget realities, board involvement, and general community perception. It served as the prelude to the distillation of *Asking Rights* into the simplified C+F+O formula, which took on the larger challenge of being able to derive funding based on the delivery of outcomes that are valued by investors.

Section 3 Introduction
Using Your Asking Rights

Using your *Asking Rights,* actually monetizing them, is the reason you have gone through this effort. After you have successfully combined the ingredients (C+F+O) into a recipe (the IDM), you are ready for the true test: whether anyone wants to eat what you've cooked.

This final section discusses how *Asking Rights* are implemented in the real world as part of an effective, sustainable funding program. The following chapters include a discussion of why some other popular funding methods are not sustainable in the long run, examples of how the ROI/outcome message is being used in today's nonprofit industry, and a comparison of the differences between traditional fundraising models and the IDM.

If you have built your Credibility by delivering Outcomes that are valued, and combined them with solid Fundraising Skills, you have already earned *Asking Rights.* You will probably be in a better financial position already, almost as a natural by-product of the combination itself. The war stories and true experiences contained in this last section shed some light on what happens every day out there in the wild and wooly world of fundraising.

Ch. 13 It's Hard to See the Forest for the Trees (Especially When Your Part of the Forest Is Burning)
Tragedy and gimmicks are not sustainable

Ch. 14 In the Trenches
Examples from the real world

Ch. 15 What to Do Six Months Before You Ask
A checklist of necessary steps

Ch. 16 Takeaways
Things to remember

CHAPTER 13

It's Hard to See the Forest for the Trees
(Especially When Your Part of the Forest Is Burning)

Everybody has a plan, then you get hit in the face.
- Mike Tyson

WHY ARE YOU READING THIS BOOK?

Perhaps you are one of the many people looking for a solution. You have tried friendraising, raffles, golf tournaments, galas and, yes, even capital campaigns run by those "professionals." You've done your best to get the right people on the board, applied for grants, and hired good people, yet your fundraising doesn't seem to be keeping pace. To add insult to industry, you turn on the morning news and hear about millions and millions of dollars raised in just days for the latest natural disaster when all you've been hearing from your prospects is how the bad economy has tightened purse strings. Then you attend a conference where the speaker gleefully brags about how his NPO raised millions with their first 5K run. No wonder it's so tough to keep up that "rah-rah spirit" for your mission and see the light at the end of the tunnel of discouraging news.

The *Asking Rights* formula was distilled from years of in-the-trenches experience after raising money for many types and sizes of organizations. And, as you know by now, it is also grew out of a need to establish an effective funding campaign without the luxury of being able to draw on years of personal relationships or big budgets for advertising that (supposedly) could stimulate demand.

Does the formula hold up when a tragedy instantly causes people to open up their checkbooks? Does the flavor of the month or the fad of the season reinforce the tenets of *Asking Rights*... or do they invalidate it?

TRAGEDY + URGENCY = IMMEDIATE RIGHTS (USUALLY)

For most organizations, *Asking Rights* take time to nurture, develop, and mature. In the case of an emergency, natural disaster, or horrific social situation, such as Hurricane Katrina or the Boston bombing, *Asking Rights* seem to be naturally and immediately conferred. While this is not always the case, the situations that do succeed in raising a lot of money in a relatively short period of time seem to stick out in our collective memories.

Why do organizations that answer the call of tragedies and emergencies seem to be granted immediate *Asking Rights*? Framing the discussion from an organizational level, in the format of the *Asking Rights* formula, provides some guidance.

Credibility

- They are often the brand name organizations that you know or with which you are at least somewhat familiar.
- They have been around a long time and often are the first to arrive in disaster or emergency situations.
- They have successfully delivered results in the past that investors value.

Fundraising Skills

- They were quick to adopt the advantages that social media offers.
- They have been raising money for a long time.
- They have the capacity to stimulate demand through big budget advertising.

Outcomes

- Since the events happen so quickly and the immediate need is so great, there is no time to develop specific outcomes or larger initiatives that can be carefully analyzed, so people look at what the organization has done in the past (see Credibility).

- Outcomes are immediate and are, usually, the basic necessities of life: food, water, shelter, and safety.

- The outcomes needed often require large scale operations or specialized skills that only certain organizations can offer.

What follows are three examples that you will undoubtedly recognize: one is international, one is large scale regional and one is more localized. All facts and figures are offered as obtainable at the time of the writing of this book. You will see the success they had, as well as how each shares the previously mentioned characteristics.

International Disaster: *Earthquake in Haiti, January 2010*

Scope of Disaster

- An unofficial report puts the death toll between 46,000 and 85,000. Haiti's government says about 316,000 died.[i]

- The cost of rebuilding Haiti's homes, schools, roads, and other infrastructure could soar to nearly $14 billion, according to a study by economists Andrew Powell, Eduardo Cavallo, and Oscar Becerra at the Inter-American Development Bank. They calculated a base estimate of $8.1 billion for a 250,000 dead-or-missing toll, but estimate this figure is likely to be at the low end and conclude that an estimate of US $13.9 billion is within the statistical margin of error.[ii]

Funding Results

- The "Text Haiti to 90999" campaign added $10 to a donor's cell phone bill. Within 72 hours of the earthquake, more than $8 million had been raised for American Red Cross relief efforts, a record amount for instant mobile giving. By early March, the Red Cross had raised more than $32 million by text.[iii]

- 60 groups and their international affiliates raised a total of $2.1-billion, including $1.43 billion from Americans, according to a *Chronicle of Philanthropy* tally.[iv]

- The Red Cross raised more money than any other charity, and has so far pledged or spent $330 million of the $486 million it received. Habitat for Humanity International has spent all of the $36.4 million it received. Food for the Poor, which, like Habitat, worked in Haiti for more than two decades before the quake, spent all of the $20.7 million it raised in the first 10 months after the disaster.[v]

- In all, more than $2 billion has been raised for Haiti relief, but the reconstruction will take years and organizations in Haiti continue to need funding.[vi]

Large Scale Regional Disaster: *Hurricane Katrina, August 2005*

Scope of Disaster

- Direct and indirect deaths: 1,833 total; 1,577 in Louisiana, 238 in Mississippi, 14 in Florida, two in Georgia, and two in Alabama.[vii]

- $81 billion in total damage with $40.6 billion in insured losses.[viii]

- University of North Texas Professor Bernard Weinstein put the total economic loss from Katrina to be as high as $250 billion, because he takes into account not just the damage, but the impact for disrupted gas production and general effect on national economic growth. For example, in 2005, economic growth as measured by Gross Domestic Product (GDP) growth went from 3.8 percent in the third quarter (July-September, when Katrina hit) to 1.3 percent in the fourth quarter (October-December, when production losses were felt).[ix]

Funding Results

- Donations to Katrina hit $1 billion in three weeks.[x]

- Habitat for Humanity's Operation Home Delivery is rebuilding 1,000 houses along the coast with the $80 million it has raised.

- Catholic Charities USA collected $142 million.

- The American Red Cross announced that it had received enough donations to cover the $2.1 billion cost of its operation and asked donors to give to other hurricane-relief groups.
- The United Methodist Committee on Relief, an arm of the United Methodist Church, raised $69.6 million.[xi]

Localized Disaster: *The Joplin Tornado, May 2011*

Scope of Disaster

- 161 lives lost due to the tornado.[xii]
- Nearly 3 million cubic yards of residential debris created; 10,746 individuals and businesses registered for disaster assistance; 19,523 claims received totaling an estimated $1.9 billion, and of that, approximately $1.49 billion in losses paid by insurance, or 77.9%.[xiii]

Funding Results

- In the past year, about $39 million in contributions and pledges have been received by many of the major organizations providing front-line assistance to tornado victims and those planning Joplin's comeback.[xiv]
- The Missouri Department of Insurance reported that insurance companies had paid a total of $509 million in claims for the damages caused by the tornado. That amount, however, did not mark the end of claims coming in from property owners and those hurt in the disaster.[xv]
- Analysts estimated that the total cost of the disaster could top $3 billion. Missouri's Insurance Commissioner John Huff estimates that the actual total will be less, coming in at $2 billion.[xvi]

Other than being tragedies, what's the common thread? Most of the appeals were heavily emotional. They had all the ingredients of successful visual advertising: images of people suffering, children in need, destroyed homes, unsanitary conditions. And they all raised a lot of money.

Am I acquiescing to the strength of the emotional appeal? Not really. These examples are a validation, not a contradiction, of the *Asking Rights* formula. They show that Credibility (track record) and Fundraising Skills (obviously) make Outcomes a fairly safe bet. The outcomes are usually focused on such a devastated area that anything is welcomed. These disasters are terribly emotional events, so it is not unusual that an emotional response is given in return. But, is this a sustainable model? Is the CEO of the Red Cross hoping that another disaster hits so he or she can balance the budget? Of course not.

Many of these organizations mentioned are designed for emergencies, disasters and unexpected events. It is part of their mission. They also have a very sophisticated fundraising plan and the heft to put it into action. They have sustainable strategies, it's just not as visible as it is in times of emergencies. Can the average NPO count on disasters for a constant funding stream? Does the average NPO want to?

GADGET PLAYS AND GIMMICKS ≠ ASKING RIGHTS

There seems to be a common fundraising practice among some NPOs: spending way too much time on everything but actually raising money. Many organizations put on great events and, to be fair, they do raise some money. Events are fun (for some) to plan, but the purpose is often lost in the shuffle of activity. These types of efforts seem to hone the skills of event planning rather fundraising, which would be a far better skill set to develop to help make the organization more sustainable. Some organizations seem to like doing this type of activity-focused funding so much that they are in a perpetual state of event planning.

A discussion of the general categories of gadget plays and gimmicks follows. Why the phrase "gadget plays and gimmicks?" Simple, they do not focus on the outcomes delivered.

1. Social Events

These include the black tie dinners, the annual galas, the silent auctions, etc. We have all been to them and, when successful, they often serve to connect patrons more closely to the organization. Yet they also take a huge time commitment from the staff and volunteers, and some cost a considerable amount of money to produce.

Many of these functions include some statistics read aloud by some well-respected people and some might include a video, but most of those attending did not buy a $100 ticket to hear statistics. Even though the host organization is attempting to capitalize on its outcomes, it is actually raising money on emotional appeals. As said to me once by a major funder at an event, "I am here for the social aspect, for fun. Come see me in my office if you want to talk seriously about money."

In defense of social events, they can accomplish some very important things.

- They may serve as events on which the community relies and to which people undoubtedly anticipate.

- They may serve as signature events for the NPO to help build its brand awareness.

- They often draw some important people and, in turn, draw others who want to be in the presence of the aforementioned important people in a relaxed social setting.

- They can more firmly connect people to the organization, capitalizing on the popularity factor in that now participants can see for themselves that many others are also committed to the cause.

- Costs can often be defrayed through sponsorships and ticket sales to the point where out-of-pocket expenses are minimal, allowing more of the funds raised to actually benefit the mission.

2. Athletic Events

While golf and tennis and bowling tournaments (oh my!) have been a staple of fundraising for as long as there have been sports, the meteoric rise of fun runs, cause walks, and competitive races that benefit charities cannot be ignored. Although these newer entrants into athletic-focused event fundraising are still a small percent of total giving in this country, hovering around 0.49 percent in 2006 and 0.51 percent in 2010, the growth in revenue of the top 10 athletic charity events from 1995 to 2010 was more than three times as fast as charitable giving in general.[xvii]

This noticeable rise of athletic events has prompted some analysis that might otherwise not have happened.

- Their indirect impact can be substantial. The Leukemia & Lymphoma Society says that its Team in Training program employs some 350 full-time people to train and organize its participants. It grew 13 percent in the recent five years when many NPOs saw revenue drop.[xviii]

- While the cost can be competitive with other forms of fundraising, it is not uncommon for 50 cents of every dollar raised to be spent on the event itself. The list of expenses is more diverse than one might think: tents, permits, security, water, t-shirts (a prerequisite apparently), signage, toilets, etc. These are costs that are rare in the social event setting.[xix]

- Chris Olivila, a University of London psychology researcher, has identified what he calls the "martyrdom effect" at play in athletic fundraising events, where several things happen.

  1. Longer distance races raise more money than shorter ones.

  2. Sponsors give more when they believe an event will be painful for their sponsoree.

  3. "…the more you ask people to suffer, the better."[xx]

3. Miscellaneous Gimmicks

Almost every nonprofit I have worked with in the past 18 years has some sort of specialized event or niche effort. Gimmick may be too strong a word but, again, if it does not focus on the value of outcomes delivered, it really is a trick play and cannot be depended on in the long term. The game plan to be adhered to is delivering outcomes.

The list of what the industry will come up with next to distract from the winning game plan (delivering outcomes) is always growing. The category already includes various raffles, cash-a-thons, coupons, shopping, dining, mouse clicking, texting, and on and on.

These efforts can be very financially rewarding, but their shelf life is always in question, hence the term "fadraising."

Some of the more interesting examples include:

- Rappelling off of 25-story buildings;

- Plane pulls, where teams pull a large jet across a tarmac;

- Polar plunges/Polar Bear Clubs, which involve icy dips in lakes or oceans during the winter;

- Dining/shopping with "friends," which in this instance means prominent people, the kind you have always wanted to meet, have dinner with, or go shopping with;

- Changes to a person's physical appearance, such as growing a beard only to subsequently shave it off when the goal has been reached; and

- Virtually any challenge that involves something uncomfortable, unhealthy, or unhygienic, such as hours without sleep, continuously touching a vehicle for days, or wearing a certain article of clothing for months.

The Internet, and especially social media, has provided some unique opportunities that did not exist a few years ago. Not only does it provide new channels to get the word out, it can make the financial transaction easier to complete as well. The texting campaigns discussed earlier in this chapter attest to that.

A STEP IN THE RIGHT DIRECTION

Certain periods throughout the year, often centered around the end of year holidays, provide a unique window to offer seemingly "once a year" opportunities to give. These examples may at first appear gimmicky, but some list outputs and others even outcomes, which serve to make us aware of just how far a dollar will go while emphasizing the efficiency of the organization (Credibility in *Asking Rights* terminology). They include:

- $3 buys a student workbook in Darfur (Catholic Relief Services);

- $12 buys 20 pounds of soap (Oxfam);

- $25 buys a "No Mo' Chemo" party (St. Jude's Children's Hospital);

- $100 buys one month of art supplies for Chinese orphans (Half the Sky);

- $150 buys one front door (Habitat for Humanity);

- $500 delivers a newborn baby in Guatemala (Project Concern International);

- $1,000 buys one month of housing and basic needs for a woman and her child/children escaping abuse in the U.S. (Global Giving); and

- $2,500 buys an operation for one child with a congenital heart condition (Children's HeartLink).[xxi]

The above list is better than typical social or athletic events in that the dollar amounts are presented as the cost to deliver specific outcomes, which speaks to the rational appeal.

The common denominators of most gadget plays and gimmicks are that they are subject to fads, require a lot of staff time, are expensive and cause the NPO to take their eye off of the ball: their mission. They certainly have their place as fun things that bring notoriety to and attention for the nonprofit, and can diversify the funding portfolio. But, at the end of the day, the organization has to ask itself whether these tactics are financially worth all those things, both positive and negative, when fully accounted.

REFERENCES

[i] ('June 1, 2011) "Report challenges Haiti earthquake death toll," *BBC News, US & Canada Section*, Retrieved on June 1, 2013, from http://www.bbc.co.uk/news/world-us-canada-13606720

[ii] (February 16, 2010) "Haiti reconstruction cost may near $14 billion, IDB study shows," *Inter-American Development Bank*, Retrieved on June 1, 2013 from http://www.iadb.org/en/news/webstories/2010-02-16/haiti-earthquake-reconstruction-could-hit-14-billion-idb,6528.html

[iii] Andrew Chaikivsky, "The Best & Brightest 2010," *Esquire Magazine*, December 2012, 124.

[iv] Marisa Lopez-Rivera and Caroline Preston Chronicle of Philanthropy (January 5, 2012). "Most Money Raised for Haiti Recovery Has Been Spent, but Needs Continue, a Chronicle Survey Finds," *Chronicle of Philanthropy*, Retrieved June 1, 2013, from http://philanthropy.com/article/Charities-Have-Spent-Most-of/130223/

[v] Ibid.

[vi] Victoria Fine (Last Updated May 25, 2011). "Haiti Earthquake Relief: How You Can Help," *Huffington Post*, Retrieved June 1, 2013, from http://www.huffingtonpost.com/2010/01/12/haiti-earthquake-relief-h_n_421014.html

[vii] (August 21, 2009). "Katrina's statistics tell story of its wrath," The Weather Channel, Retrieved June 1, 2013, from http://www.weather.com/newscenter/topstories/060829katrinastats.html

[viii] Ibid.

[ix] Kimberly Amadeo, "How Much Did Hurricane Katrina Damage the U.S. Economy?" *About.com*, Retrieved on June 1, 2013 from http://useconomy.about.com/od/grossdomesticproduct/f/katrina_damage.htm

[x] Jacqueline L. Salmon and Leef Smith (February 27, 2006). "Two-Thirds of Katrina Donations Exhausted," *The Washington Post*, Retrieved June 1, 2013 from http://www.washingtonpost.com/wp-dyn/content/article/2006/02/26/AR2006022601383.html

[xi] Ibid.

[xii] Public Information Office (Last Updated May 14, 2012), "Fact Sheet - City of Joplin, May 22, 2011, EF-5 Tornado," Retrieved June 1, 2013, from www.joplinmo.org/

[xiii] Ibid.

[xiv] Connie Farrow (May 26, 2012). "About $39 million given to major funds for Joplin's storm recovery," *The Joplin Globe*, Retrieved June 1, 2013 from http://www.joplinglobe.com/topstories/x1968172487/About-39-million-given-to-major-funds-for-Joplin-s-storm-recovery

[xv] Marc Christopherson (July 27, 2011). "Missouri Department of Insurance says Joplin disaster will be the most costly insurance payout in state history," *Insurance News Report*, Retrieved June 1, 2013, from http://www.liveinsurancenews.com/missouri-department-of-insurance-says-joplin-disaster-will-be-the-most-costly-insurance-payout-in-state-history/854253/

[xvi] Ibid.

[xvii] Anne Kadet, "Heartstrings, Purse Strings," *Smart Money*, December 2010, 62.

[xviii] Ibid.

[xix] Ibid.

[xx] Guy Raz. Interview with Alix Spiegel. "Why Do We Give? Not Why or How You Think." All Things Considered, NPR, November 25, 2011.

[xxi] Tim McKeough, "Wanted," *Fast Company*, December 2010/January 2011, 94-95.

CHAPTER 14

In the Trenches

*There is not a difficulty to having an insider's
knowledge and an outsider's mind. The more you
understand, the better off you are.*
- Jerry Brown

NECESSITY BREEDS CHANGE

The two sides of the debate on ROI and its usefulness for nonprofits used to be whether or not it was appropriate. After many years of banging my drum that it was not only absolutely appropriate, but necessary for financial sustainability, the ROI-based approach is finally being viewed as acceptable. The differences in the discussion are now more subtle, and they tend to gravitate towards how a more value-oriented approach is actually implemented in fundraising activities.

Because my clients are all over the country, I am almost always competing against a local firm for a fundraising campaign. My competition always has the home-court advantage. To help them gain additional advantage points, they will say things like:

- We have been keeping a database of who has money in this town for years;

- We have gotten money from (insert usual suspect) for many of our clients; and

- We know who has come into money, gotten divorced, sold their company, etc.

This familiarity is a good thing and sometimes I wish I had it when engaging with a new community. But the truth is, when the usual suspects see this traditional fundraiser coming, they often run the other way. They've seen them enough. It doesn't seem to matter who the new client is, the fundraiser feels that each new client deserves some of the prospect's money and the methods to get at it are usually the same.

This is how relying on an ROI approach actually got started. I did not have the local contacts to fall back on so I had to lead with something different. And that difference was ROI, value propositions, and answering "What's in it for me?" for the investors.

This is just one of the differences in how my colleagues and I approach the actual, what-we-do-when-we-go-to-work-every-day fundraising campaign. The next section illustrates some of the other differences in how we implement successful campaigns.

SERIOUS CAMPAIGN DIFFERENCES

So far in this book, I have been fairly critical of the emotional camp, websites that report numbers not outcomes, the nonprofit sector in general for being somewhat disconnected from funders, and traditional fundraisers. As a reminder, the major differences between old school/traditional fundraisers and those of us who embrace *Asking Rights* and the IDM are:

1. Emotional appeal vs. rational appeal;
2. Who makes the ask;
3. Campaign structure; and
4. A focus on outcomes delivered.

The Appeal

Chapters 3 and 4 went into detail about why a more rational ask may be a better avenue to success than a purely emotional version. Emotional appeals are the primary tool of traditional fundraisers, and obviously they have worked in the past. The operative phrase here is "in the past."

Part of the reason the industry evolved this way may have been one of tradition, possibly decorum, maybe even a bit of "if it ain't broke, don't fix it." Times have surely changed, and I believe that the nonprofit industry will be better off for it. Let me add a slight twist on the controversy between the emotional versus rational appeal.

When proponents of the emotional ask concede some ground, they often do so with the following caveat: "Use the emotional appeal to get in the door and use the rational appeal to get more money." This might be true, but is a rather small bone to throw to the rational camp.

This concession completely disregards the fact that some people will become connected to the organization because of its ROI! Just like the analogy that some people buy a car based on color or aesthetics while others base their decision on horsepower and towing capacity, some people will become connected to the organization, and will be more likely to invest substantial dollars, based on the value proposition they are offered.

Even better is that when an NPO does not have a connection (versus concern or capacity) and needs to establish one, it can use ROI/impact/value as the avenue to do this. When new sources of funding are the goal, the rational approach is more often than not the perfect vehicle to accomplish it. The connection to the organization can be *because* of the ROI/impact/value proposition, rather than just icing on the cake.

The Heavy Lifting

This is a nice way of saying "Who really makes the ask?" and is the easiest category of all to point out stark differences in approaches. Typically, and for years and years, the traditional fundraisers have relied on volunteers — board members, staff, and previous benefactors — to actually do the work in what is commonly referred to as a volunteer-driven campaign. And by work, I mean who is doing the preparation (i.e. research on prospects, customized proposals, etc.) and actually meeting with people about making an investment in the organization.

Their process goes something like:

1. Traditional fundraiser gets hired by organization.
2. Traditional fundraiser scripts and choreographs what should be said to prospects.

3. Traditional fundraiser rehearses with an appropriate volunteer what needs to be said, how to answer questions, and how to overcome objections.

4. Traditional fundraiser sends volunteer out into the world, armed with pledge cards and scripts, to ask his/her friends and business acquaintances for money.

This approach relies almost exclusively on peer-to-peer leverage. The person doing the asking must be someone respected by the askee, and should be invested at the same level or preferably higher. Does it work? Sure, but volunteer-driven fundraising inherently unburdens the dreaded ask from the professional fundraiser and instead puts it on volunteers, who by definition are not professional fundraisers.

News Flash: Volunteers (often) have day jobs. And they almost always have a personal life. Very few have understanding employers that permit them the luxury of time to dedicate to going around to all of their friends and business acquaintances to ask for money on behalf of the NPO. Many also do not want to jeopardize a personal or professional relationship by pushing too hard during an ask. Since they are relying primarily on their relationship and rapport with the prospect, the appeal tends to be primarily an emotional one, not a rational one.

Would I rather give to a nonprofit when someone I know asks me? Sure. But when given the choice between a nonprofit that I believe is doing good things and a nonprofit that I know nothing about but am being asked by someone I know, I will take the effective, familiar nonprofit every time. This was the conclusion of the material presented in Chapter 5. Relying on the asker, rather than the reason, seems to fly in the face of a rational person: it implies that the personal relationship is more important.

Campaign Length

Because I do not rely on volunteers to do my work, my campaigns are typically measured in months, not years. Every day I am asking for money on behalf of my clients. I'm getting them the financial support they need faster and, at times, in greater sums than expected so they can fulfill their mission.

Many old-school fundraisers find this reality difficult to comprehend. They usually attribute our success only to the fact that our campaign model utilizes a full-time effort. Dedication and focus do, at times, bring about results more quickly, but that's only part of the reason. The more important point is that volunteer-driven campaigns take so long precisely because they rely on volunteers to do the asking. Volunteers typically can only dedicate some of their time (rarely, if ever, even part-time) to the effort and, frankly, it's work they do not really like to do because they feel it exploits their relationships. The combination of no available time and reluctance to risk relationships can spell trouble for a campaign. It's no wonder why those 10 pledge cards the traditional fundraiser gave them sit on the corner of their desk for months and months.

Case Statement

There are many examples in the public domain about how to write a Case Statement. And there are some good pointers in those examples, I'm sure. But, to put this matter in perspective, I cannot recall any campaign in the last 18 years where a dime has been raised on the mission statement of an organization. I believe it was Nancy Lublin, CEO of Do Something, who said something along the lines of mission statements are when you torturously wordsmith your board into consensus... about something that doesn't really matter anyway. From a fundraising context, I couldn't agree more.

Having said that, every one of my campaigns has a Case Statement or, as I prefer to call it, a Case for Investment. Rather than focus on an organization's history, background, the mission, vision, etc., I tend to focus on the program of work, the initiative for which money is being sought in support. Of course, I always save the most ink for the *outcomes* of the program of work.

FILLING THE VACUUM OF EFFICIENCY

It is becoming more popular, and in some cases even fashionable, to "sell" impact instead of good ol' fashioned fundraising. In a tip of the cap to traditional fundraising, those who have actually raised money know it's not about selling.

One of the extensions of this concept is the formation of a Social Capital Market, proposed by some as a place where "good" can be monetized, which then tacitly assumes an "efficient market." Efficient markets, in the financial arena, are a theoretical way to describe how capital markets (the stock market) work. It is often used by Wall Street professionals to defend their ways of doing business, usually by convincing the public that you need them to keep the playing field level and not get left behind. An efficient market assumes, among other things, that 1) all information is known by everyone, 2) the information can be understood by all, and 3) the information is free of cost. There is debate as to whether capital markets are efficient or not. There is no debate as to whether the nonprofit market is efficient: it is not.

What fills the void left by the lack of efficiency is called fundraising.

Let's be realistic. Even with the proliferation of online websites with various ratings and scores, buyers (read: funders) of nonprofit "goods" do not have all the information they need. And, sadly, as of this book's writing, outcomes are still not usually a part of the myriad amounts of information available online.

A FEW WAR STORIES

The following stories are real. The names were changed to protect the innocent, but all details are true.

We Will Even Drive Them to the Meeting

I know the traditional fundraisers' group well. Not only do I compete against them for clients, I have worked with them on projects. In one example that I have retold many times, I was hired by an organization that chose to hire both my company and a large, well-known, traditional-as-they-get fundraising company. At one point, the client asked us to differentiate our approaches to the inner circle of the organization. I explained how my company relies on an investment-based approach, and that we do the ask.

The word "ask" was a bit confusing to this group, so I explained what it really meant, driving home the point that my team and I are present for the conversation with a prospect and take full responsibility for making the ask for funding. I told them we don't place that burden on a volunteer, potentially putting a relationship at risk.

The traditional fundraiser piped in: "We are involved too. We will even drive you to the meeting." What was not said is that, yes, they will drive the car, but they won't get out of it and they won't go in with the volunteer. Their reasoning? It will detract from the peer-to-peer dynamic. I have many a happy client who will attest that no detraction takes place.

Going Through the Motions

Someone once said that fundraisers are only a small step ahead of used car salesmen in that they will say anything to make the sale/separate you from your money. Many people think this is standard procedure for how fundraisers approach potential funders on behalf of their client. I want to instead focus on what some fundraisers will say to prospective clients in order to get hired as fundraising counsel.

I was once presenting on the topic of fundraising at a conference attended by nonprofits focused on caring for the homeless. After my presentation, an NPO executive director came up and told me that her organization had just concluded a feasibility study done by a traditional fundraiser. This fundraiser recommended moving forward with a campaign for $1.2 million after completing approximately 25 interviews. She asked if I thought that was a good estimate of funding potential.

My first response was that I had no idea. I did not know anything about their constituency, how connected they were, their program of work, their outcomes, etc., etc. What I really didn't know was their C, F or O. I did make the point that 25 interviews were really not too many — I customarily do at least twice that per study — and that there are some rules of thumb regarding individual indications that might point to the legitimacy of the $1.2 million estimate.

She said she had been given no information on individual indications, not even a range of possible investment. With no detail as to how this fundraiser got to the $1.2 million estimate, it raises the question as to whether this number is based on casual conversations, or even blind guesses, by the fundraiser. (For more on this, see *The Money Question* in Chapter 15.) She then told me that she had subsequently gone to her two largest potential funders, who were supposedly interviewed by the fundraiser during the study, and asked about their possible support. What she learned was almost beyond belief: their combined potential investments alone totaled more than $1.2 million. With just two of the 25 people interviewed by the traditional fundraiser, the nonprofit was (almost) guaranteed to surpass the recommended goal!

This story suggests the traditional fundraiser:

1. Either did not know how to do a real feasibility study,

   or

2. They lowballed the number so later on they would look like heroes for exceeding the goal.

To make matters worse, she said the proposal they presented to her for continuing their services had them spending the first four months developing the Case Statement. Whether through inexperience or unscrupulous practices, their suggested course of action would cause the campaign to lose valuable momentum. Once lost, momentum is hard to regain.

Not Enough Information

I have to be very careful on this one, but it is one of the best war stories I can share. My company was conducting a feasibility study for a recreational facility in the middle of the country. With 10+ interviews behind me, I was ready for the pivotal one, the one that would make it very difficult to move forward if this person said "not interested." The community was very small, so word would get around if this person said "no," and there weren't a lot of second choices for campaign leadership.

We already knew this project was going to have the name of a prominent judge on the building because of his elevated standing in the community, even though he was not going to be the largest investor. There were also some delicate personal and professional connections between the person I was about to speak with and this judge, which is not unusual in smaller cities.

After an interesting discussion about the merits of the project, the prospect and I got to the part about potential financial support. The answer shocked me: "no." I was not going to let him off that easy, so I asked why. "Because the person whose name is going to be on that building shot my daddy." I swear to you, I can't make this stuff up. I didn't know whether to look concerned or roll with what could easily have been a joke. I went with the former.

So I blurted out, "Are we talking about the same person? I am talking about Judge So and So." The response, "That's why he didn't go to jail for it; he's a judge."

When I returned to the client's office later that day, they were, of course, anxious to hear about my meeting with this gentleman. After explaining what transpired, I asked them how this little nugget of information was not known to them. "Of course we knew that," they explained, "we just don't like to talk about things like that."

The story did, though, have a happy ending. When all of the skeletons were brought out into the daylight, the funds were raised and the facility was built.

COMMUNICATING OUTCOMES IN THE REAL WORLD

Over the years, I have run across some interesting examples of how nonprofits try to communicate their outcomes. Some are more successful than others, but all certainly grab your attention (or, at least, they grabbed mine). I have included some of the more interesting here.

Example #1

Arena:	*Environmental*
Message Communicated:	*The value equivalent of your investment*
Medium Used:	*Insert in monthly power bill*
Organization:	*Tennessee Valley Authority*

Exhibit 14.1 Outcomes Example #1

Example #2

Arena:	*Human Services*
Message Communicated:	*Track record, efficiency*
Medium:	*Place mat on food tray*
Organization:	*Ronald McDonald House*

Exhibit 14.2 Outcomes Example #2

187

Example #3

Arena: *Pet welfare*

Message Communicated: *Extent of problem*

Medium: *Magazine advertisement*

Organization: *Morris Animal Foundation*

Exhibit 14.3 Outcomes Example #3

Example #4

The following exhibits are all from the same nonprofit. This organization merits more than one example because they produced one of the best reports on communicating the value of outcomes I have ever seen.

Arena:	*Domestic Violence*
Message Communicated:	*Value of outcomes*
Medium:	*Impact report*
Organization:	*Harbor House of Orlando*

First, in Exhibit 14.4, they list national numbers that some good Internet research would produce. This is secondary research, not primary, but sets the stage well. They also list some broad local impacts and costs. Then, in Exhibit 14.5, they list outputs, lots and lots of outputs. Lastly, they list the value of outcomes in Exhibit 14.6, some of which are targeted to different motivations, but all tied to how investors think.

I think you will see why I feel this is one of the best examples of communicating all of the things that traditional logic models require: programs/activities, outputs, outcomes... and then goes the extra mile to demonstrate the value of those outcomes. The sheer volume of information and activities also connotes Credibility, one of the essential elements necessary to establish *Asking Rights*.

Exhibit 14.4 Broad Outputs and Outcomes

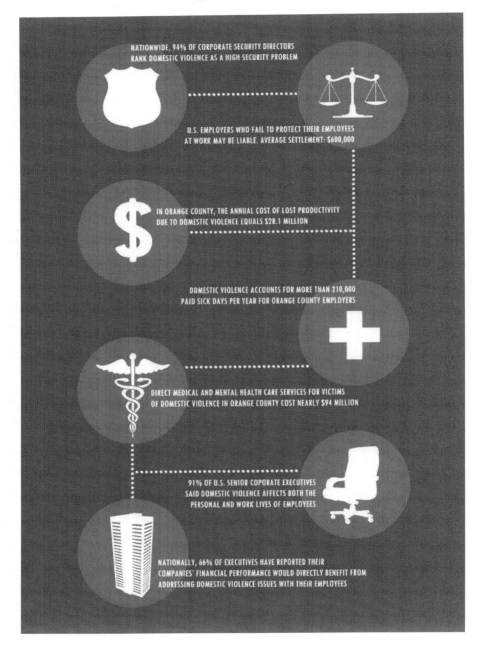

Exhibit 14.5 More Outputs

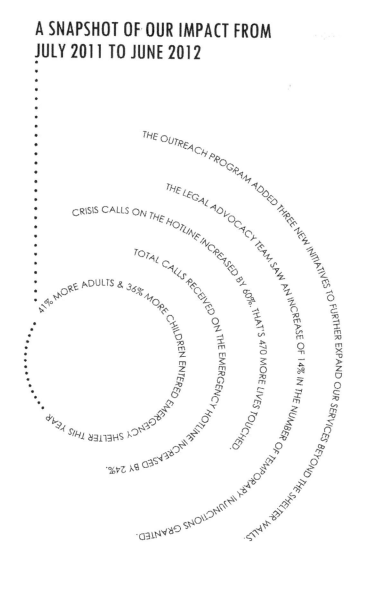

A SNAPSHOT OF OUR IMPACT FROM JULY 2011 TO JUNE 2012

THE OUTREACH PROGRAM ADDED THREE NEW INITIATIVES TO FURTHER EXPAND OUR SERVICES BEYOND THE SHELTER WALLS.

THE LEGAL ADVOCACY TEAM SAW AN INCREASE OF 14% IN THE NUMBER OF TEMPORARY INJUNCTIONS GRANTED.

CRISIS CALLS ON THE HOTLINE INCREASED BY 60%. THAT'S 470 MORE LIVES TOUCHED.

TOTAL CALLS RECEIVED ON THE EMERGENCY HOTLINE INCREASED BY 24%.

41% MORE ADULTS & 36% MORE CHILDREN ENTERED EMERGENCY SHELTER THIS YEAR

Exhibit 14.6 Value of Outcomes

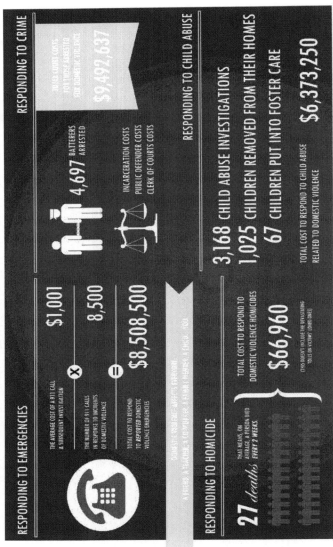

RESPONDING TO EMERGENCIES

THE AVERAGE COST OF A 911 CALL & SUBSEQUENT INVESTIGATION **$1,001**

⊗

THE NUMBER OF 911 CALLS IN RESPONSE TO INCIDENTS OF DOMESTIC VIOLENCE **8,500**

⊜

TOTAL COST TO RESPOND TO *REPORTED* DOMESTIC VIOLENCE EMERGENCIES **$8,508,500**

RESPONDING TO CRIME

THAT'S OVER EIGHT AND A HALF MILLION DOLLARS FOR THESE ARRESTED FOR DOMESTIC VIOLENCE **$9,492,637**

4,697 BATTERERS ARRESTED

INCARCERATION COSTS
PUBLIC DEFENDER COSTS
CLERK OF COURTS COSTS

RESPONDING TO HOMICIDE

27 *deaths* THAT MEANS, ON AVERAGE, A PERSON DIED *EVERY 2 WEEKS*

TOTAL COST TO RESPOND TO DOMESTIC VIOLENCE HOMICIDES **$66,960**

(THIS DOESN'T INCLUDE THE DEVASTATING TOLLS ON VICTIMS' LOVED ONES)

RESPONDING TO CHILD ABUSE

3,168 CHILD ABUSE INVESTIGATIONS

1,025 CHILDREN REMOVED FROM THEIR HOMES

67 CHILDREN PUT INTO FOSTER CARE

TOTAL COST TO RESPOND TO CHILD ABUSE RELATED TO DOMESTIC VIOLENCE **$6,373,250**

TOTAL COST TO ORANGE COUNTY TAXPAYERS

$24,441,347*

*CALENDAR YEAR 2011

DOMESTIC ABUSE COSTS EVERYONE.

CHAPTER 15

What You Must Do Six Months Before You Ask

...the easiest !*#!$%* thing in the world is to convince people not to write a check.

- Sean Penn

STEP #1   GET YOUR HOUSE IN ORDER

When large amounts of money are the goal, nonprofits usually think capital campaign. And while capital campaign used to mean bricks and mortar, it has come to represent a dedicated effort that seeks larger dollar levels regardless of the intended use. My guess is that this bricks-and-mortar connotation came from the accounting profession, where funds were raised for capital, depreciable assets. It now signals multi-year pledges, more supporting customer involvement, and months, or even years, of effort.

While a capital campaign structure is not the only funding vehicle where *Asking Rights* can be put to good use, it is the most effective for several reasons.

1. It is the most cost-effective method of raising money per dollar spent for the average nonprofit, normally in the range of 10 percent or under.[i]

2. It puts the organization directly in front of potential investors, in a face-to-face situation, which allows for immediate (positive and negative) feedback, course correction, and negotiation.

3. It provides the best opportunity to explain outcomes.

Annual campaigns, events, and grants do not have these advantages. Isolated asks, as part of an ongoing development effort, do offer these same advantages, but lack the dynamics of a true campaign, which uses momentum, leveraging, and recruiting to help bring about success.

Up to now, we have talked about *Asking Rights* as a process, a school of thought that focuses on delivering outcomes, and using it as the cornerstone of a sustainable funding plan. Now we move to more of a managerial or operational perspective, and the major steps in mounting a successful funding effort.

In a 2007 article for *AOL Small Business* entitled "The 6 Biggest Mistakes in Raising Startup Capital,"[ii] Brad Sugars discusses the process of raising money for a for-profit venture. Interestingly enough, the first three missteps can be applied directly to many small NPOs doing their first capital campaigns.

1.   Half-Baked Business Plans
2.   Focusing Too Much on the Idea and Too Little on the Management
3.   Not Asking for Enough Money

The business plan, in this case, is the campaign plan. Unfortunately, many nonprofits are just not realistic when it comes to understanding how long things may take, how much they might cost, and how much effort they require. They also tend to fall in love with catchy campaign names, tag lines, and the promotion of the effort. While this may be fun and exciting, it is no substitute for getting up in front of people and asking for money. The last point can potentially involve the most costly mistake: they often do not ask for enough money. As mentioned before, everyone calibrates to the leaders in a campaign, so if the early investors are not at the appropriate levels, no one else will be either. Add to that the fact that potential investors' schedules are tight and it often takes time or multiple attempts to get on their calendar for a meeting, and there is rarely the opportunity to ask twice if an organization leaves money on the table the first go-round.

These mistakes are the more obvious and dangerous pitfalls when launching a capital campaign. There are also some subtle points that can just as easily have negative consequences that should be considered.

Vernacular

One highly suggested change, besides redefining what a capital campaign can mean, is to eliminate the phrase "capital campaign" entirely.

Substitute "strategic" for "capital" and "initiative" for "campaign."

The reasoning is simple. Just think of the last time the words "capital campaign" were mentioned to your board. Did their eyes light up in anticipation? Did a small cheer go up? Was the enthusiasm palpable? Of course not! They remember what capital campaign meant the last time: more work for them, the type of work they dislike to begin with, and, in some instances, failure to reach the goal.

Strategic implies strategy. Something well thought through. Something that may have taken months to discuss and reach consensus. Initiative implies something new. Something other than the status quo. Capital campaign implies asking their friends for money... after they have already opened up their own checkbook.

Within the organization, the word campaign will undoubtedly be used. For the purposes of this book, I have used the word campaign consistently. But for positioning in the eyes of the public, "strategic initiative" will be met with much more support.

Cash Flow

Why do 50 percent of new companies fail within the first five years? Because they are undercapitalized. Why do many campaigns fail? Because they are undercapitalized. Yes, it's important to have the right ingredients, use the right recipe, and understand the customer. These things will earn *Asking Rights*, but campaigns do not cash flow themselves, which often comes as a complete surprise to nonprofit management.

Investments received during a campaign will not start materializing until four to six months after the kickoff and few investments will be on schedule as an organization might ideally like, which includes not being compatible with the fiscal year or in preferred lumpier amounts. In rare cases, the collection of investments can be accelerated, but it has to be planned for from the beginning. On average, organizations should have four to six months of cash to pay outside counsel, print collateral material, and cover meeting/travel costs.

Realistic Staffing

Campaigns are work. Lots of it. Some organizations, by virtue of their size and lack of development staff, almost certainly have to hire outside counsel. Other organizations, even those with a development staff, choose to hire outside counsel for the specific skills these professionals bring. Internally, an organization may be focused on its annual campaigns or events (very common) without time or personnel to spare, so when personal asks are needed, they hire time and experience.

Staffing needs, though, go beyond the obvious. Those making the ask are easy to spot, but the support people are just as important and are often overlooked in the plan. When an organization is shelling out precious resources for high-powered help, those people should be out of the office, in front of people, doing what fundraisers do best. You don't want to pay to have them sit behind a desk, spending their time scheduling appointments, arranging meeting space, or dealing with general logistics. If these high-powered professionals are good at what they do, significant amounts of new activity will be generated and the support staff needs to be in place in order to capitalize on it.

Asking Rights Components

By now, the importance of the components of *Asking Rights* are obvious. But from a managerial perspective, consider how they are approached.

Credibility

This is one that a professional fundraiser should not be expected to magically produce for an organization. Yes, they might be able to help package and present it but, ultimately, this comes from the organization's current and past performance, from visible staff, and from the board. It takes a long time to develop and should ideally be in place before a campaign begins.

Fundraising Skills

A realistic assessment of an organization's ability to raise funds is critical. If an organization is still utilizing the old-school model where volunteers do all the heavy lifting, outside counsel will do just that: counsel you. This begs the question: does your board have the necessary skills? Does your staff have what is needed? As an executive director/CEO, do you have the necessary skills (or the time)?

Outcomes

Outcomes will likely need to be refined, demonstrated, and put in the language of investors. This should be the focus of the Case for Investment. Outside assistance is often needed to do this, but please resist the urge to hire the economics professor at the local college or university to do it. There is a reason why we do not hire them in our company as fundraisers: they are great with the quantitative side of things, but typically bad with relating the results to the intended audience.

STEP #2 CONDUCT THE NONNEGOTIABLE FEASIBILITY STUDY

Before any strategic initiative is launched, a feasibility study must be conducted. Period. This is the first step of the IDM just expressed in a different way.

1. **Discovering Investor Motivations**
2. Translating Your Outcomes to Value
3. Matching Your Value to Investor Motivations
4. Using Campaign Dynamics to Maximize Funding

Why am I so hard-nosed on conducting a feasibility study? Tell me, do any of the following statements sound familiar?

"We already know we are going to do a campaign, why waste the time and money to do a feasibility study?"

"Let's save the money we would spend on a feasibility study and put it towards a campaign."

"We know a campaign is feasible, we just need to determine how much."

If these statements have floated around your board meetings, or if you have found yourself saying them, you are missing the point of what a feasibility study really accomplishes.

Why is it nonnegotiable? Here's why.

1. It's a *cultivation* step, not a solicitation step. The first time you meet someone is not the time to ask them for money. In a feasibility interview, the possibility of asking them for a financial commitment is taken off the table. A study allows for true conversation and an exchange of information. It is the time to pique interest, listen to opinions, and gather information that can be used later to secure investments.

2. Input is vitally important. You want people's opinions on the program of work, the budget, the leadership of the organization, and the outcomes expected. You also want to understand situations as they relate to future investment potential, including timing, decision making authority, and anything else that may be a speed bump in the process.

3. Another important point regarding input: it is not a survey! It is a conversation, often with long answers that don't neatly fit into choice A, B, or C. The better the conversation, the more that is learned that can be used later during the actual campaign to gain investments from those who offered their input.

4. Ownership. This is the first chance to help potential investors put the program in their own words, which leads them to begin thinking of the initiative as *their* initiative. It won't likely happen in one meeting, but that first meeting is one of the best chances to fertilize the ground for future growth. When investors take ownership in an effort, it has a

much higher chance of succeeding. Put another way, as it has been said to me by a campaign chairman, "It is my program, and I will not let it fail."

The Money Question

There is one more area of the feasibility study that merits discussion: the money question. By this I mean the question about how much money a person might be inclined to invest in the proposed program. You are not asking for a commitment at this time, but for an indication of support.

I include this specific point because so often, unfortunately, it is glossed over. Without an answer to this question, a feasibility study is incomplete. You may have gathered lots of input, cultivated the entire town, and even gotten well down the path of ownership, but without answering the money question, you are no closer to an estimate of true funding potential than when you started.

Here's an insider's secret: the people you are interviewing know why you are there. You told them why you were coming. They are the caliber of people who have been through this drill before. If they did not want to talk to you, they would not have given you the time of day, much less taken time to discuss something in which they were not interested. Technically, they have already invested money in the initiatives you are proposing, because time is money, so to not get to a more definitive answer would be unprofessional. Even if that answer is "no," the information this prospect has shared during the meeting undoubtedly has provided clues on how to potentially turn that "no" to a "yes" during the campaign.

STEP #3   USE WHAT YOU JUST LEARNED

Now you have feedback from potential investors. You know what they like, what they don't like, and what they have the propensity to fund. It's time to begin steps two and three of the IDM.

1. Discovering Investor Motivations
2. **Translating Your Outcomes to Value**
3. **Matching Your Value to Investor Motivations**
4. Using Campaign Dynamics to Maximize Funding

Think of it. You now have tested your program with many of the people that you will ask to pay for it. You let potential investors do a test drive. Did they like it? Did they love it? Did they like some parts and hate others?

Since investors will not agree with everything you put in front of them during the feasibility process, you will likely need to reprioritize, massage budgets, and reconfigure programs to make the initiative more palatable. In other words, your program of work moving forward will need to reflect the investor's motivations for funding. This is known as the program refinement stage, and it is the rare occasion when budgets do not need to be realigned, or some elements emphasized less and others more.

But what if the response was predominately negative? You then have four choices.

1. You can change your program of work and move forward.

2. You can change your budget and move forward.

3. You can do some combination of the above and move forward.

4. You can choose to not move forward.

What to do? These questions may help you determine the answer.

- Was the response due to your outcomes or the funding needed to accomplish them?

- Were outside factors, unrelated to your outcomes, the reason for less than positive responses? These might include timing, budget cycles, prior commitments, the economy, etc.

- Can you change what you are asking to be funded to better match what investor's value without compromising your mission?

- Did anything surface that you need to work on before you launch a campaign?

- Is the door open to come back with a revised program of work?

STEP #4 USE CAMPAIGN DYNAMICS / LAUNCH A CAMPAIGN

Typically, the feasibility study will take two months and then the board will take a month to digest the information and make a decision. Add to that what is necessary during the early stages of a campaign and, realistically, an organization has six months of work from campaign idea to making the first ask.

1. Discovering Investor Motivations
2. Translating Your Outcomes to Value
3. Matching Your Value to Investor Motivations
4. **Using Campaign Dynamics to Maximize Funding**

After a well-executed feasibility study, you are now armed with all of the information needed to launch a successful campaign, assuming the response was positive enough. While an organization does not have to launch a campaign to take advantage of the benefits of either *Asking Rights* or the IDM, a campaign is the best way to maximize those benefits.

As presented in Chapter 10, those campaign dynamics are:

- Peer-to-peer leverage;

- Calibration to leaders;

- Sequential asks (top down/inside-out process); and

- Ownership.

Without a campaign, the process becomes a series of individual, often isolated asks, which can limit or stymie synergistic campaign dynamics. In other words, these dynamics (or lack thereof) are most apparent when an actual campaign is launched.

In addition to the four IDM components, two other campaign ingredients must be mentioned: leadership and evaluation. While we are now dancing close to describing the mechanics of a campaign, which is not the intent of this book, I would be remiss if I did not mention these components and their place in any successful initiative.

Leadership

Enlisting the right leadership in a campaign is vitally important. They become the face of the campaign and lead with their own investment, sealing the fate of the entire effort, either for better or for worse. This is why the first months of the campaign are devoted to this cause. Second chances are usually not given in the pursuit of leadership, so you need to get it right the first time.

Evaluation

Evaluation refers to asking for the right amount of money from the right prospect. If the ask amount is not appropriate and lead pledges come in at levels lower than necessary to set the right pace for the initiative (since everybody calibrates to the leaders), then the entire campaign could be in trouble. This domino effect can have negative consequences that are difficult to recover from, but can be prevented with the correct evaluation process.

The four to five year cycle of funding, presented as a capital campaign/strategic initiative in this chapter, has not yet shown any signs that it can't be repeated over and over. I have personally worked with some organizations that are on their fifth successful campaign cycle. The reason they are able to do this is based on only one thing: they consistently deliver outcomes that investors value.

REFERENCES

[i] J. M. Greenfield, *Fundraising Cost Effectiveness: A Self Assessment Workbook* (1996), 281.
[ii] Brad Sugars (September 20, 2007). "The 6 Biggest Mistakes in Raising Startup Capital," *Entrepreneur*, Retrieved July 25, 2013, from
http://www.entrepreneur.com/article/printthis/184350.html

CHAPTER 16

Takeaways

Worldly wisdom teaches us that it is better for reputation to fail conventionally than to succeed unconventionally.

- John Maynard Keynes

The above quote may, at first, seem counter to the unconventional theme of this book. Mr. Keynes' comment was made in reference to the portfolio managers of the world, whose reputations were more likely to be left intact if they put your money into safe (as in a blue chip company) investments, even though they might fail. Better to fail on a conventional stock, which all would consider a prudent investment, than to succeed by making risky investments in small, unknown companies.

The same phenomenon can be observed in the world of fundraising. Many nonprofits seem happy to launch a volunteer-driven campaign based on emotional appeals and come up short, rather than to risk failing by trying something different, despite the fact that it has had much success.

By applying the concepts in this book: the investor's perspective, their motivations, and alternatives to traditional fundraising (and why they may work better), *Asking Rights* prepares you to be much more successful in asking people, corporations, and foundations for funding. By earning *Asking Rights*, your organization should be more firmly on the road to sustainable funding. Because you and your funders view the act of giving money to your organization as an investment, rather than as a donation, certain outcomes are expected to be delivered. This is the beauty of the Investment-Driven Model: if their investment pays off, they are much more likely to continue to be investors. You have earned the right to again ask them for funding.

10 THINGS TO REMEMBER
(IF YOU REMEMBER NOTHING ELSE)

1. Not everyone has *Asking Rights*.

   They are earned, not given just because you are a nonprofit.

2. Everyone is capable of developing *Asking Rights*.

   It just takes effort and an organization-wide commitment.

3. There is more to *Asking Rights* than just asking for money.

   Even though the IRS says you can ask people for money, it does not mean you will be successful at it.

4. *Asking Rights* are not static.

   They change and can become more powerful or less powerful over time.

5. Those that have *Asking Rights* make their value obvious.

   These organizations stand apart from the ones that don't and will have a smoother road to sustainable funding.

6. It's more about the right outcomes being valued than how the value is determined.

   It's not how good your aim is, but whether you are aiming at the right targets.

7. Rational appeals made on outcomes delivered are more sustainable than appeals made on emotions alone.

   Outcomes are why people ultimately invest in nonprofits, time and time again.

8. The right ingredients are important.

   Credibility + Fundraising Skills + Outcomes all need to be present.

9. The right recipe is important.

   The right ingredients must be combined in the right way to maximize your funding potential.

10. An investor's motivations are different than a donor's.

    Ignore this at your own peril.

A BIT OF LEVITY

Years ago — we're talking the early 1980s — when I was a whitewater rafting guide in northern Wisconsin, I lived for a time in a cabin. While it did not have running water, it did have a few shelves of books that served to broaden my horizons. One of those was *The Executives Coloring Book,* a lampooning look at young executives and their climb up the corporate ladder to the boardroom. Years later, I happened to see one posted for sale on EBay for more than $80 and it finally struck me that simple, humorous pictures can many times get the point across better than hundreds of pages of words.

In 2010, I published *The Traditional Fundraiser's Coloring Book.* Sensing that the world might not be ready for such a frontal assault on certain sacred cows, I published it anonymously. It is presented through the eyes of a traditional fundraiser, an outside consultant who has been hired by a typical nonprofit.

As a parting message, I share with you Exhibits 16.1 and 16.2, the two pages from the coloring book that are most applicable to the theme of this book. The traditional fundraiser depicted is uncomfortable with the concepts and tenets we have discussed, and seems to be happy with the status quo. My hope is that you are not.

Enjoy!

Tom Ralph

Exhibit 16.1 The Traditional Fundraiser's Favorite Words

THESE ARE MY FAVORITE WORDS. I use them all of the time.
They make the client feel warm and fuzzy. They make me look like an expert.

Copyright © 2010 ColorTheTruth.com

Exhibit 16.2 Unfamiliar Territory

THESE ARE THE WORDS MY COMPETITION USES. They scare me.
I don't know what they mean.

Copyright © 2010 ColorTheTruth.com

INDEX

4

401(k), ix

A

Acorn, 53, 55, 56
Ahern, Tom, 29, 34, 40
altruism, 59, 143
American Red Cross, 167, 168, 169, 170
Andreoni, James, 31
Andresen, Katya, 58, 69
annual campaign, 18, 30, 65, 196
Ariely, Dan, 60
Askee. *See* the ask
Asker. *See* the ask

B

B Corporation, 45
Bayesian prior, 70, 76, 77
beneficiary, x, 45, 50, 51, 141
Berresford, Susan, 92
Better Business Bureau, 75, 96, 103
Blue Chip, 53, 55, 56
board, 16, 25, 39, 50, 62, 64, 70, 74, 97, 98, 105, 106, 108, 124, 125, 138, 151, 152, 154, 155, 158, 160, 161, 162, 165, 179, 181, 195, 197, 198, 201
branding, 109
Buffett, Warren, 32
Burgess, Timothy, 57, 69
buyer-donor, 49

C

C+F+O, 95, 113, 119, 162, 163
calibration to leaders, 137, 201
capacity, 13, 14, 52, 59, 75, 79, 80, 87, 126, 136, 156, 166, 179
capital campaign, 16, 18, 24, 32, 35, 38, 39, 46, 55, 88, 124, 135, 165, 193, 194, 195, 202
Case Statement, 181, 184
Catholic Charities USA, 168

Catholic Relief Services, 173
charity, 1, 7, 20, 21, 22, 29, 33, 40, 52, 58, 60, 68, 70, 79, 80, 121, 168
Charity Navigator, 70, 74, 75, 81
Charting Impact, 75, 100, 101, 103
Cheney, Dick, xii
Child Fund International, 31
Children's HeartLink, 174
Chronicle of Philanthropy, 7, 14, 34, 56, 68, 69, 78, 81, 167, 174
community investment, 22
Congress, 10
Convergent Nonprofit Solutions, vii, 146, 161
corporate giving, 22, 61
Corporation for National and Community Service, 82, 84
Credibility (*Asking Rights* component), 77, 106, 107, 108, 109, 113, 114, 115, 116, 117, 119, 137, 163, 166, 170, 173, 189, 196, 204
customer-donor, 48, 50, 51
Cygnus Applied Research, 67

D

Davis, Shai, 58, 69
delivering outcomes, xiv, xv, 40, 144, 172, 194
Donation Impact Calculator, 108
donor(s), x, 1, 4, 5, 6, 8, 9, 11, 17, 20, 31, 32, 34, 46, 48, 49, 50, 51, 52, 53, 59, 61, 67, 68, 70, 74, 78, 79, 88, 91, 96, 100, 122, 167, 169
donor proposition, 45, 50
donor value proposition, 50, 51, 42
Drucker, Peter, 50, 96, 97, 98, 103, 144

E

Edna McConnell Clark Foundation, 83
EEV. *See* explicit expected-value
emotional appeal(s), ii, x, xvi, xvii, 1, 10, 28, 29, 30, 40, 46, 51, 54, 55, 56, 117, 119, 122, 143, 171, 178, 203
Ethonomics, 23
evaluation, 110, 202

evaluation(s), 74, 83, 84, 86, 103, 105, 109, 110, 124, 137, 201, 202
expected value, 76, 87
explicit expected-value, 76, 77

F

fadraising, 173
Farsides, Tom, 33
Fast Company, 23
feasibility study, iii, iv, 98, 99, 106, 114, 122, 124, 145, 183, 184, 197, 198, 199, 201
financially sustainable organization, 28, 35, 37
Five Steps to Demonstrating Value, 102
Food for the Poor, 168
Ford Foundation, 92
Ford, Gerald, xii
Form 990, 70, 74
fund development, 135
funder(s), i, ii, v, xv, 1, 4, 5, 9, 16, 17, 18, 19, 50, 51, 54, 72, 74, 77, 78, 79, 86, 87, 98, 99, 100, 102, 103, 115, 118, 127, 144, 145, 146, 147, 150, 152, 155, 156, 160, 171, 178, 182, 183, 184, 203
funding campaign, 145, 165
funding models, xi, 141, 142
funding strategy, 37, 135
Fundraising Skills (*Asking Rights* component), 106, 107, 109, 114, 115, 116, 117, 119, 163, 166, 170, 197, 204

G

Gates Foundation, 32, 40
gift(s), ix, x, xi, 4, 6, 17, 20, 34, 49, 59, 60, 61, 65, 88, 121
GiveWell, 49, 70, 76, 77, 81
Global Giving, 174
Goodwill Industries, 108
Grace, Kay Sprinkle, 135, 138
Greene, Robert, 43, 44
GuideStar, 70, 74, 75, 81, 100

H

Habitat for Humanity International, 168
Haiti, 167, 168, 174, 175
Half the Sky, 174
Harbor House of Central Florida, 128, 129, 139, 189
Heart, 53, 54, 56
Hurricane Katrina, 166, 168, 175

I

IDM. *See* Investment-Driven Model
Impact Investing, 45
Independent Sector, 75, 96, 100, 103
Inter-American Development Bank, 167, 174
Interpersonal Skills, 110
investable outcomes, xi, 10
Investable Outcomes, ii, 95, 118, 119, 126, 127, 128, 129, 131, 134, 139, 146
Investment-Driven Model, ii, 95, 118, 119, 121, 122, 139, 141, 142, 143, 146, 147, 163, 197, 199, 201, 203
investor, i, xi, 4, 5, 6, 9, 10, 11, 12, 13, 20, 25, 32, 48, 49, 50, 51, 52, 53, 71, 72, 73, 92, 99, 113, 117, 118, 122, 123, 126, 127, 130, 131, 134, 148, 155, 156, 166, 184, 200, 203, 205
investor-donor, 48, 49, 50, 51

J

Jobs, Steve, 48
Johnson, Bob, 161

L

Laffer Curve, xii, xv
Laffer, Arthur, xii
leadership, 105, 106, 108, 109, 110, 114, 132, 137, 138, 154, 184, 198, 201, 202
letting outcomes drive, 135, 136
Leukemia & Lymphoma Society, 172
leverage investments, 110
Levitt, Stephen, 60

Limited Liability Low Profit Company, 45
List, John, 32, 35, 38
Lublin, Nancy, 23, 26, 181

M

Mahajan, Sanjoy, 92, 93
Management by Objectives, 144, 145
marketing campaigns, 1
matching grant, 110
MBO. *See* Management by Objectives
measurement and evaluation, 83
metrics, 80, 87, 88, 89, 90, 91, 92, 93, 122
mission, ii, ix, xi, 4, 11, 12, 13, 25, 30, 50, 68, 74, 80, 83, 89, 96, 98, 103, 114, 117, 124, 126, 127, 130, 131, 143, 153, 165, 170, 171, 174, 180, 181, 200
Morino Institute, 86
Morino, Mario, 83, 86, 93
Motivational Pyramid, 79

N

name-brand nonprofit, 28
NPO, 118, 135, 138, 147, 151, 165, 170, 171, 174, 179, 180, 183

O

Olivila, Chris, 172
Oppenheimer, Danny, 31
Organizational Value Proposition, ii, 42, 46, 68, 72, 102
Outcomes (*Asking Rights* component), 106, 107, 109, 111, 114, 115, 116, 117, 119, 137, 163, 166, 170, 197, 204
outputs, xiv, xv, 16, 25, 84, 91, 111, 130, 173, 189
OVP. *See* Organizational Value Proposition
Oxfam, 173

P

Panas, Jerold, 59, 60, 69
peer-to-peer leverage, 136, 180

Penna, Robert, 20, 117
people give to people, iii, xvi, 29, 65, 66, 136
Philanthrocapitalism, 44
Philanthropedia, 74, 75
philanthropy, 6, 40, 69, 81, 174
Poniewozik, James, 71
Potomac Knowledge Way, 86
primary customer(s), 16, 45, 51, 84, 86, 98, 99, 111
Project Concern International, 174

R

rational appeal, xvi, xvii, 1, 28, 33, 38, 44, 51, 53, 55, 56, 62, 67, 68, 69, 143, 174, 178, 204
return on investment, vii, xi, 9, 11, 16, 24, 25, 34, 39, 42, 44, 45, 46, 47, 49, 71, 72, 73, 77, 83, 87, 92, 102, 119, 122, 123, 134, 146, 149, 152, 155, 156, 159, 163, 177, 178, 179
Robin Hood Foundation, 83
ROI. *See* return on investment
ROI for Nonprofits: The New Key to Sustainability, vii, 6
Rokia study, 31, 34, 36, 37, 47, 65
Ruby, Rebecca, 58, 69
Rumsfeld, Donald, xii

S

Salvation Army, ix, 6
Saul, Jason, 50, 56, 102, 146, 148
Save the Children, 31
self-interest, 43, 44, 59, 60, 128, 143
Shooting Star, 53, 55, 56
Sierra Club, 32
SIF. *See* Social Investment Fund
Skoll Foundation, 88
Slipka, Brigid, 45, 49, 50
Social Actions, 74, 81
Social Capital Market, 182
social events, 25, 171
Social Innovation Fund, 82, 84, 93
social investment, 24
social return, 24, 25
SocialEdge.org, 88, 93
societal issues, ii

solicitation, ii, 25, 66, 71, 75, 77, 78, 147, 198
SRIO. *See* social return
Stanford Social Innovation Review, 56, 134, 139, 141, 142, 148
Stanford University, 64
strategic initiative, 195, 197, 202
Sugars, Brad, 194, 202
sustainable funding, i, xi, xii, 1, 20, 21, 29, 37, 87, 106, 107, 121, 163, 194, 203, 204

T

Tactical Philanthropy, 49
tax-exempt status, ix
the ask, 16, 18, 39, 71, 103, 109, 111, 112, 136, 137, 146, 178, 179, 182, 183, 196, 202
The Committee Encouraging Corporate Philanthropy, 22
The Money Question, 184, 199
The Nonprofit Outcomes Toolbox, 20, 117
Translating outcomes into value, 125

U

United Methodist Church, 169

United States, ii, 10, 61
United Way, 32
University of Chicago, 35, 38
University of Sussex, 33

V

valuable outcomes, xii, xv, 1, 55, 87
value proposition(s), 13, 28, 38, 44, 45, 47, 50, 51, 53, 72, 75, 77, 83, 87, 89, 102, 141, 146, 178, 179
Venture Philanthropy Partners, 83, 86, 93
VillageReach, 49

W

Wall Street, 182
Wall Street Journal, 7, 14
Weinstein, Bernard, 168
What's in it for me?, 48, 60, 69, 119, 143, 178
Wise Giving Alliance, 75, 96, 100, 103

Z

Zak, Paul, 60

31437403R00135

Made in the USA
Lexington, KY
11 April 2014